HOW TO CATCH SALMON

ADVANCED TECHNIQUES

Charles White and Guest Authors

Illustrations by Nelson Dewey

First Printing 1974
Second Printing 1978
Third Printing 1981
Fourth Printing 1986
Fifth Printing 1989
Updated Edition 1992
Reprinted 1995

Canadian Cataloguing in Publication Data

Main entry under title:
 How to catch salmon: advanced techniques

Reprint. Originally published: Sidney,
B.C.: Saltaire Publishing, 1974.

ISBN 0-919214-65-7

1. Salmon-fishing. 1. White, Charles,
1925- II. Dewey, Nelson.
SH684.H69 1992   759.1'755   C91-091763-9

Heritage House Publishing Company Ltd.
#8, 17921 - 55 Avenue
Surrey, B.C. V3S 6C4

Printed in Canada

THE AUTHOR

Charlie White is an internationally known author, film maker, television personality, and fish behavior researcher.

He has written nine books on salmon and marine life, with sales over 400,000 copies, making him among the leading authors on salmon fishing. His latest book is *Charlie White's 101 Fishing Secrets.* His first book, *How to Catch Salmon: Basic Fundamentals,* has sold more than 130,000 copies. He is co-author of a new university textbook, *Fisheries: Harvesting Life from Water,* being used for courses at the University of Washington and other colleges.

In addition, he developed a series of Underseas Gardens marine exhibits in the United States and Canada where the public can descend beneath sea level to watch sea life in a natural environment.

In 1973, he began experimenting with a remote-controlled underwater television camera to study salmon strike behavior. His underwater close-ups, in freeze frame and slow motion, revealed for the first time many fascinating new facts about how salmon and other species approach and strike various lures.

He has made three feature-length films about his work, two of which are now marketed on video cassette (*Why Fish Strike* and *In Search of the Ultimate Lure*). He has been recognized in *Who's Who* for his fish behavior studies. He has also invented a number of popular fishing products, including the Scotty Downrigger, Electric Hooksharp, Perfect Picture Lures and Formula X-10 fish-feeding stimulant.

Articles on Charlie have appeared in major magazines and newspapers across North America. He also has his own television series and is a frequent guest on radio and television talk shows. His TV series, Charlie White's Fishing Machine, is seen across Canada, in Turkey, England, Hong Kong and many public stations in the U.S. In addition, he conducts fishing seminars at colleges and in auditoriums throughout the Pacific Northwest and lectures several times a year at the University of Washington School of Fisheries.

Charlie lives on the waterfront near Sidney, B.C., and continues his unique underwater research on fish strike behavior. For more information write Charlie at 11046 Chalet Road, Sidney, B.C. V8L 5M2

Contents

Very Important

Do not go fishing without first studying the current B.C. Tidal Waters Sport Fishing Guide, published annually by the Federal Department of Fisheries and Oceans. It is available free at sporting goods stores, marinas and similar outlets. The Guide contains all current regulations governing sport fishing not only for salmon but also for halibut, rockfish, crabs, oysters and other species. Check carefully the sections on spot closures which were introduced as a conservation measure. In addition, remember that size limits apply to all salmon.

INTRODUCTION

This volume is intended primarily for anglers with several years fishing experience or for those who have read and put into practice the information in our best-selling basic book, *How to Catch Salmon—Basic Fundamentals.* It explains the fundamentals which any angler needs to know before he can catch salmon with reasonable skill and some consistency. Subjects covered include description of salmon species, choice of tackle, fish intelligence, preparing lures, finding salmon, trolling patterns, landing fish, and much more.

This book covers more detailed techniques and methods used by seasoned anglers, especially when the fishing is "tough," as it seems

to be most of the time in recent years. It is full of tips and secrets used by the experts to find fish and tantalize them into striking when the average fisherman gives up and relaxes with his bottle of beer, settling for a pleasant boat ride.

One of the best means of becoming aware of the problems of the

average fisherman is to teach a night school class on the subject as I have for over 20 years. A few real beginners will enroll, but the vast majority are weekend anglers with a full set of tackle and a small boat. They feel very frustrated at their lack of success and are very tired of the heckling from family and friends when they come home empty-handed. As one Spanish immigrant told me: "Many times I have gone out for ze appointment with ze fish, but ze salmon never keeps ze appointment!"

IT'S THIS CRAZY "DAYLIGHT SAVING" TIME-- GETS ME ALL CONFUSED!

Most students have never read any salmon fishing books, and those who have do not realize the importance of following the basic rules outlined. This attitude shows up especially when we go on

7

field trips. For instance, not one fisherman in ten bothers to sharpen his hooks each time he starts out! This omission alone probably costs him several salmon a season when a slashing fish grabs a dull hook and it slides harmlessly out of its mouth.

Check Lure Action

Even more important is strict attention to the lure itself and its proper action in the water. Time and time again the amateur strips out line without first testing lure action beside the boat. This testing

must be done each time a lure or bait is placed in the water. If the lure is working properly, Mr. Salmon may be interested. If not, nothing else matters — you won't catch anything!

Most Difficult Problem

Finding salmon is often the most difficult problem for a fisherman, particularly the weekender. There are many times when even the experts are skunked. Following a few common sense suggestions, however, will increase your chances three- or four-fold.

Instead of wandering aimlessly around the fishing grounds, you

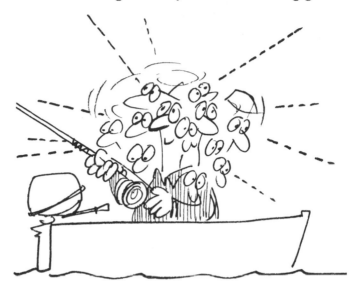

should have a definite fishing plan at all times. Keep your eyes and ears open to what is happening around you. Look for seagull and diving bird activity, follow tidal currents and back-eddies, watch what successful anglers are doing and quiz them on lures, depth, and other pertinent facts.

While we don't want to cover material already explained in detail in our first book, my experience shows that many fishermen continue to ignore many of the fundamentals even after being exposed to them. For this reason, I hope that repetition of a few basic rules will strike a responsive chord with readers of this book.

Until fishing fundamentals become a regular habit and are done almost automatically, the material in this book will be of limited value. There is no point in learning the secrets of the experts if you don't know the ground rules. After all, you can't learn trick diving unless you first know how to swim.

My more diligent fishing students often call me several months after completing the course to report proudly on their successes. If they have absorbed the basic rules, they will have a new feeling of confidence when they go out for a day on the water.

Most, however, will also admit to some frustrating days when the fish just wouldn't bite or when others caught fish and they

AH — THAT'LL BE
GRIDWELL
CHECKING IN...

didn't. "Now that I've pretty well mastered the basics," they will say, "how long will it take to become a real expert?"

"The rest of your life," is my reply. Although there is a moment when many fishermen realize they are beyond the beginner stage, this happy state usually occurs when they begin to catch fish because they did certain things, rather than just blundering into a fish occasionally. The transition from this point, however, is a gradual process that takes forever.

This is what makes fishing the delightful sport that it is. Psychologists claim that happiness comes more easily when you are growing and learning. Fishing is a continuous learning experience.

No one knows all the answers! This open-ended educational process is the common denominator in all the great sports and hobbies, including golf, tennis, chess, bridge and photography, to name a few.

So much for philosophy and general background. If you feel that you know the basic fundamentals, this book should give you a good start on that long road to becoming an expert, known in fishing language as a "top rod" or "high liner."

I'm still moving along that road myself and have found the material prepared by Ken McDonald, Lee Straight, Dan Stair, Rex Field, and the other outdoor writers to be very helpful. In fact, editing this material has introduced me to a lot of techniques I'll be trying on future trips.

My own fishing expeditions usually range from Victoria to Nanaimo with a summer trip to Barkley Sound. If you see my 23-foot Bayliner Trophy Fisherman with C-*Quest* emblazoned on both sides, pull over and say hello. We'll compare notes and perhaps we can both learn something.

Good luck and Good Fishing,

Charlie White

CHAPTER ONE   By Charlie White

General Fishing Lore

Although we have tried to segment this book into chapters for easy reference to specific techniques, there is a great deal of general information which defies such pigeonholing. We think such facts and practices are of such importance that we have placed them right up front. Without this general information, many of the subsequent details don't make nearly as much sense.

When dealing with a quarry that lives in a world almost completely alien to us, we develop fishing techniques by trial and error. Even then our conclusions are based almost entirely on circumstantial evidence. Except on rare occasions near the surface, we don't see the salmon actually take our lure — and even then, it is often just a blur, swirl, and splash. So we don't really know even how it strikes, let alone why.

Very often, we can't tell whether or not a salmon has even seen our lure. If we knew that the fish had seen and rejected our offering, we could take corrective action. Now we can only speculate. Maybe the fish see our bait and turn away or perhaps follow it for closer inspection. Does one in three "lookers" grab the lure or is it only one in 20 or 50? Knowing the efficiency of our various baits would take much of the guessing out of fishing.

My own experiments with an underwater TV camera are designed to shed some light on this mystery. I can watch the salmon look at the lure and study its behavior as it strikes or turns away. Some of the findings have surprised me, notably the large number of fish that look and turn away.

Lots of fish nip at the bait or bump it. This action made me realize the importance of sharp hooks. Sharpening to "sticky sharpness" has doubled my catch and led to the development of the Hooksharp Electric Sharpener.

Fisheries Departments in Oregon, Washington and British Columbia are gathering a growing amount of data on the habits and needs of salmon. But these studies are still in their infancy. They are dealing with a creature that is born and dies in fresh water where they have some control over it, but which spends most of its life roaming the largest ocean in the world where they have no control.

It is hard enough to study an underwater creature when you can keep it in an area where you can watch it. Trout and bass at least remain, or can be kept, in a location with defined boundaries. While

some data is now building up, we don't even know where the big ocean feeding salmon live during an important phase of their life cycle. This is the time when they attain their greatest growth, when they feed most voraciously. As sports fishermen, we are vitally interested in knowing more about this active feeding time. Knowing how, when, and why they eat helps us design and work our lures to take advantage of these habits. Here, again, specific knowledge would help us ring the salmon's dinner bell.

FINDING SALMON

Before we can entice fish to strike our bait, we must first find them. Indians, commercial fishermen, charter boat guides, and keen sportsmen have all contributed to the considerable fund of knowledge on how to find salmon. Looking for surface activity and interpreting its meaning is one prime way to zero in on feeding schools of fish. Bait fish milling on the surface is a hopeful sign, but herring or candlefish boiling frantically out of the water is a sure sign of something feeding on them from below.

Diving birds, (murres, murrelets, auklets, etc.) might be pushing up the feed. Fortunately, you can determine very quickly if they are present since they seldom stay under water for more than a minute. If there are no divers, then the bait is being attacked by salmon, dogfish, rockfish or lingcod. Salmon or dogfish are the most likely prospects, but you may have to troll through the bait to determine which one unless you see the telltale fin of the shark-like dogfish.

Watch Herring
Herring or candlefish "ball-ups" (where baitfish instinctively gather together in a tight round ball of living flesh) are another sure sign of feeding predators. The herring try to get to the center of the ball while the birds or fish slash away at the luckless ones on the outside surface. The predators also push right through the ball-up. I can remember vividly watching a huge sphere of small herring with no attackers in sight when suddenly a large dogfish appeared from in-

side the herring ball. He swam almost lazily into the clear, his jaws dripping with half-eaten carcasses.

Schools of surface feed and ball-ups are usually, but not always, spotted first by the hungry eyes of nearby seagulls. They cruise most fishing areas like a fleet of patrol planes, watching for signs of food from their high vantage point. When they spot something, they dive

to investigate, then squawk the news loudly if they find bait fish. I've always wondered why they make this raucous noise since it attracts the rest of the flock which sometimes muscle in and steal the catch of the original scout. It must be an instinct designed for survival of the group as a whole.

Gulls Informative
Watching seagulls will keep you informed on any meaningful surface activity, especially important when fishing for the shallower-feeding cohos. After spotting some feeding gulls, you must then determine what they are eating. The late Rex Field, for years the resident fishing genius at Comox, B.C., gave me some fascinating information on what can be learned from watching feeding gulls.

When you see a large gull being chased by another, according to Rex, you can be pretty sure that the herring are large, probably six to seven inches. How can you draw that conclusion? Well, the big herring can't be swallowed easily, even by the large gulls, so they often

get stuck halfway down. One gull chases another — to steal the herring right out of its mouth!

Small herring or candlefish are easily swallowed, so there is seldom any chasing by the larger birds. The small gulls are almost always feeding on these smaller baitfish since they have too much trouble handling larger sized food. If small birds are just sitting on the surface, pecking under the surface, it means concentrations of tiny shrimp or shrimp-like organisms.

Knowledge of the size of baitfish is vital information if we are to be successful anglers. If we can't actually see the bait jumping, or in the mouth of a gull or diver, Rex Field's tips can help determine bait size. Matching this size is important. Feeding salmon seem to prefer lures of the same general size as the feed they are working at the time. Their instinctive striking urge is more easily triggered by a lure which looks like one of the herring they may have wounded. They may not even recognize a lure of a different size.

Depth Gauge
Birds can tell you how deep to fish, according to Rex Field. If gulls are the only birds present, feed is just below the surface. If small diving birds (murrelets, most likely) are with the gulls, the baitfish will probably be 15 to 25 feet underwater. The murrelets will force the feed up to the surface periodically where the gulls can have a meal. However, since they don't push deep running herring all the

way to the surface, the gulls won't hang around. It follows, then, that diving birds alone mean bait is quite deep, often 100 feet or more.

Other experts use birds in slightly different ways to determine fishing depth. Jim Gilbert, third generation professional guide, graduate biologist and Fisheries Advisor, says that he has timed the

GULLS ONLY

GULLS AND
DIVING BIRDS

DIVING BIRDS
ONLY

15 to 25
Feet

To 100 Feet

divers under water. By counting how long the birds remained under, he developed estimates on relative depths to find salmon.

Fish Intelligence

As we discuss in *How to Catch Salmon: Basic Fundamentals,* fish are stupid creatures with absolutely no thinking or reasoning ability. Frustrated anglers give them credit for figuring out all sorts of things to outwit the poor fisherman. Nonsense! Salmon live entirely by instinct. Their whole life cycle is determined by a series of pre-programmed behavior patterns which evolved with the species.

They strike at a lure because a "trigger" in their tiny brain is ac-

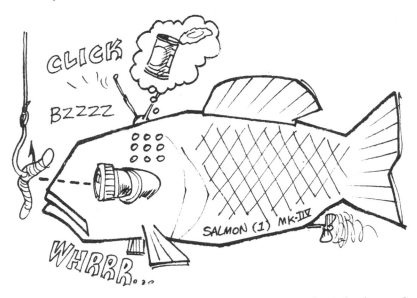

tivated by a certain sight, sound, or smell. They don't look at a lure and say to themselves, "Is that really a herring or is it a fake?" If your lure doesn't trigger the strike reaction, it might just as well be a piece of driftwood. The salmon just doesn't recognize it. There may be an initial "bite" stimulus, but upon closer inspection some other survival instinct turns it off.

So matching bait size helps get more strikes. A salmon feeding on small herring may not trigger at all when a big seven-inch bait

comes rolling by. At other times, it may grab the bigger lure. This is one reason why it is helpful to examine stomach contents of the fish you catch. It will tell you the bait the salmon are naturally feeding upon at that time.

Sometimes size is not very important; on other occasions, it can be critical. If salmon are working on a school of candlefish (needle-fish, sand lance), it is often vital to match the shape as well as the size of the feed. The long, narrow spoons, bucktail flies, or flashtails

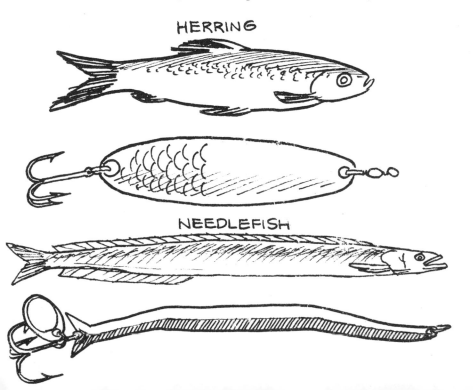

HERRING

NEEDLEFISH

will take fish, especially cohos, in this situation, while a wider spoon of the same size or color will be completely ignored.

Shrimp

What can you do when the feed is tiny shrimp? You can't match their ant-like size with any natural or artificial sea-water lure. This situation is often a tough time to catch salmon since they tend to gorge themselves on these plentiful and easy-to-catch delicacies. If no gulls are sitting and pecking at the shrimp, you can often see little V-

shaped ripples moving beside your boat. You can't always see the tiny shrimp at the apex of the ripple, but they are usually the cause.

You can't match their size, but you can try to imitate their color and perhaps the general action. Bucktail flies, flashtails, hoochies, or other "hairy" or flutter-tail lures are usually most productive at these times. Pink, ginger, red, or shades of grey approximate the color of most shrimp-type feed.

FOOD CHAIN

The food chain is the basis of all life in the oceans and some understanding of it will help catch more fish. The chain starts with microscopic plankton which can be either plant or animal, algae being the

basic plant plankton. The term plankton is also applied to many tiny animal forms, including the larvae of many larger marine creatures. (Crab larvae are often abundant in June. Since cohos will feed actively on them, a slump in catch is the consequence.)

Because plankton are the base of the whole food chain, their abundance determines the numbers of larger creatures which can sustain life. The Pacific Northwest corner of the United States, up the British Columbia coast and around Alaska is one of the richest ocean areas in the world. The relatively heavy rainfall and large river systems pour a continuous supply of rich minerals and nutrients into

the sea. This nourishment, combined with sunlight and favorable water temperatures and currents, provides ideal plankton habitat.

Plankton don't have much, if any, power of locomotion and are at the mercy of the tide and currents to carry them around. Tidal back-eddies create natural gathering places for plankton since they are swept into these areas out of the main current. They circle around in the back-eddy or just settle there. These plankton con-

centrations attract larger organisms, which in turn attract the herring and other baitfish. Foraging salmon usually quickly locate the bait.

For this reason, salmon fishing is often best in areas where such back-eddies form — off points of land, behind islands, near reefs and

sharp drop-offs, or near narrow passes between islands. When you can't see surface activity to guide you to the fish, such spots are first choice, especially with chinook since these larger salmon are not feeding on the surface nearly as often as the cohos.

Vertical Eddies
Sometimes the eddy is vertical rather than horizontal. The water pours over a shallow reef, sand bar, or shelf and rolls down and

SATURNA
ISLAND

TUMBO
ISLAND

around behind it, creating the same plankton and bait gathering conditions as with a horizontal eddy. The edges of the eddy are not as clearly defined, but a boiling, or "welling-up," can be seen in such areas.

Back-eddies can be so large it is hard to recognize them except from a low flying plane. The whole area east and north of Tumbo Island is a huge eddy when the tide floods around Saturna Island into the Strait of Georgia. A similar big backwater forms off the south end of Whidbey Island in Puget Sound.

Plankton Movements
Rex Field had some interesting thoughts on why the salmon sometimes move out into the center of the Strait of Georgia. The big tides with their large rise and fall cause fast currents which push the plankton and feed close to shore and in quieter water behind such places as Hornby Island. By contrast, with smaller tides, plankton drift more freely out into the center of the Strait and the salmon follow.

Size of tide change is also helpful in determining fishing depth. Fish are lazy just like any other animal. They won't work if they don't have to. If they don't hide in a slower-moving back-eddy during a fast running tide, they tend to move closer to the bottom where current speed is less.

This is one of the reasons why salmon tend to feed better as slack tide approaches. As water movement slows, baitfish and salmon find it easier to swim around to look for food. They also tend to move nearer the surface. With salmon at various depths and on the move, your chances of catching fish are obviously improved.

Speaking of depth, cohos are often found in the top 30 feet of water. However, my recent downrigger fishing tests have disclosed cohos at surprising depths. We hooked a beauty early one July morning at 85 feet in an area where we thought the cohos were almost always shallow. We have had a similar experience at Active Pass where we used to get them right on top. Incidentally, a coho hooked deep on a downrigger usually explodes out of the water in a

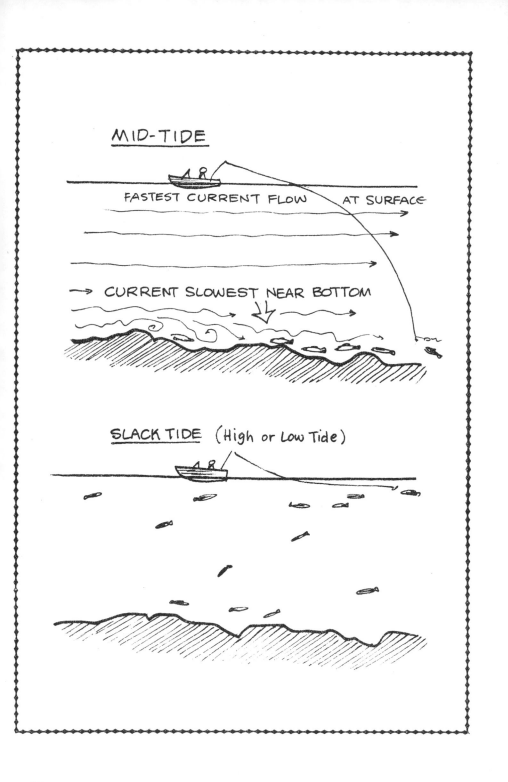

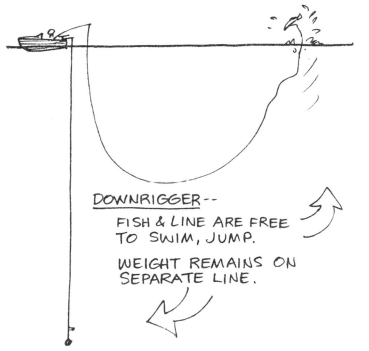

DOWNRIGGER --

FISH & LINE ARE FREE TO SWIM, JUMP.

WEIGHT REMAINS ON SEPARATE LINE.

spectacular jump after a rush from the bottom. That's one of the advantages of downriggers — after the fish trips the release, there is nothing to hold it down.

Deep Running Cohos
Perhaps a new race of deep running cohos is evolving. The shallow running fish are the ones most likely to be caught by the nets and lures which extend down from the surface. If deep running salmon are the ones that get to the spawning grounds for generation after

generation, their progeny are also likely to be deep fish. Nature's law of survival of the fittest indicates that, in this case, man-made pressures are modifying the cohos' habits.

The same thing seems to be happening to the already deep running chinooks. They are being caught deeper than ever, especially by commercial fishermen who are catching very large chinooks down 500 feet or more. Sportsmen are also going to unusual depths with mooching gear, wire lines, or downriggers. Some reports indicate sport-caught chinooks are being taken at 250 feet.

WHY FISH STRIKE

There are many theories on what triggers the instinct to strike, but the most sensible, in my opinion, is the predator analogy. Through all of nature's realm, predators have one basic function — to weed out the weak, sick, or inefficient members of their target species.

Wolves and cougars stalk the elk and deer herds, watching for the weak or young ones that get separated from the main group. If they attack the healthy ones in desperation, they often have an unhappy time. An old-time trapper told me the story of how he watched a hungry wolf pack attack a healthy bull elk. The elk shook the wolves off its back, and kicked and gored them until they slunk away in defeat.

Similarly, a government biologist mentioned watching a flock of

ducks where one duck was faltering and falling out of the formation. A large hawk appeared suddenly and headed straight for the straying duck. It actually bumped into a healthy duck, but ignored it and went on to catch the weakened one. These incidents illustrate the built-in programming of predators to attack the injured members of any group.

While salmon will prey on anything they can catch, herring, anchovies, candlefish, shrimp, and squid make up most of their diet. When they encounter a huge school of feed they slash through it, their mouths wide open to catch all they can jam into their gullets. Their explosive attack usually injures other baitfish, and their wounded struggles trigger further attacks.

Many anglers believe the salmon deliberately try to injure the

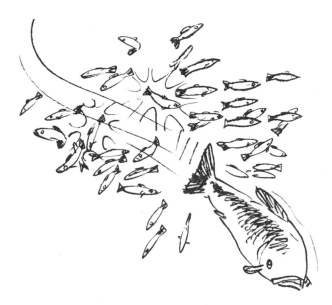

baitfish, then circle back to eat them. Watching my underwater camera has convinced me otherwise. They try to catch the baitfish on their first attack, and baitfish are injured incidentally in this attack, as they are during baitfish attacks by diving birds.

When we troll, cast, or mooch our lure among a school of thousands of bait fish, we don't have much chance of attracting the salmon unless our bait is conspicuous. We make it so by giving our lure the erratic action of a wounded herring. The salmon sees it, its

predatory instincts flash a signal, and wham — it grabs our lure in the midst of thousands of healthy herring. We hope!

GET CURRENT DATA

With the extreme unpredictability of salmon fishing, the most valuable information you can have is current data, hot from the landing net. It tells you what the salmon are doing right now.

One of the few advantages of the increasing numbers of boats is the information they can provide. When another boat catches a fish, you should find out as much as possible to guide your own efforts. Most proficient anglers are proud of their skill and are pleased to share their knowledge.

When I see a salmon landed, I try to manoeuvre near the suc-

cessful boat. After congratulating the angler, I quickly ask the pertinent questions:

    1: **What did you catch it on?** I follow-up with questions on color, size, etc., if the first answer is too general.

    2: **How much weight were you using?** This gives you only a general indication since many factors affect lure depth. However, this weight knowledge when combined with information on line length and speed (question three) will be of real help in zeroing in on the fish. Wire line equipment also affects depth, but you can often get an idea from observing the type of rod and reel used. Downriggers, of course, are easily seen and the angler will probably give you a depth in feet direct from the downrigger recorder.

    3: **How much line out?** He will reply in terms of feet or in "pulls" (about 18 inches). By this time you will be getting too far away for effective communication, although you should also know the trolling speed. The easiest way to find it is to pace yourself beside the successful boat since one skipper cannot tell another about trolling speed with any accuracy. Engine speed means nothing, with the tremendous variation in horsepower, hull shape, and other variables.

Such sharing of information makes good sense. Fresh-water anglers, fishing resident trout or bass, are often secretive about their

FRESH WATER

methods. This secrecy may be justified in some instances because there are only so many fish available in the lake or stream. If the expert tells too many people how to get them, there will be none left for himself.

Luckily, salt-water conditions are different. We are all unhappy about the declining salmon sport catches, but pleasure fishermen aren't the cause of it. Commercial interests take over 90 per cent of

SALT WATER

the total salmon caught and get first crack at the most eager biters with their thousands of trollers and wall-to-wall nets.

Sportsmen working a run of salmon will take only a portion of the school. The migratory fish move off in a short time anyway, so the expert loses nothing by helping others catch more fish.

LURE COLOR

There is mounting evidence that fish can distinguish a wide variety of colors. We don't know very much about why they prefer one shade over another, but there seems little doubt that they can differentiate between even minor color differences.

Research experiments at Brown University showed that goldfish can be trained by color codes. The fish had to bump colored targets with their noses to obtain food. They quickly learned to hit the

proper target color, even when it was switched to different positions.

Fishing salmon with bucktail flies requires a wide color selection for consistent success. Quite often, the cohos will take only one color combination, completely ignoring all others. Bucktailers formerly relied on green and white, and blue and grey flies exclusively for feeding cohos (not in river-mouth areas). Now the color selection has widened considerably. A very successful fly in recent years has been a "Fuddle-duddle" — a combination of purple and pink.

Experts have apparently conflicting theories on which colors to use under different conditions. Bucktail expert Bruce Colegrave suggests light colored flies for dark days and dark colored flies for bright days. Hoochy experts, on the other hand, find that light colors are best for sunny days and dark colors work best on dark days. Freshwater bass experts tend to agree with the latter theory. Their experience suggests bright color on a bright day, dark color on a dark day. (See Heritage House book, *Bucktails and Hoochies*, by B.C. experts Bruce Colegrave and Jack Gaunt.)

One of the few situations where there is general agreement is matching color of the natural food in the area. This matching means green and white, or blue and white, in schools of herring or candlefish, or shades of pink in concentrations of certain types of shrimp.

But we don't know, however, how water color, reflection, or depth affect what the fish sees. What may look purple to us may

look blue or black to a salmon underwater. Maybe this condition accounts for the success of the new reflective lures.

Twinkle-skirts probably started this trend. At first glance, these thin strips appear to be colorless, clear plastic. Moving and turning, they reflect back every color of the rainbow — blue, pink, green,

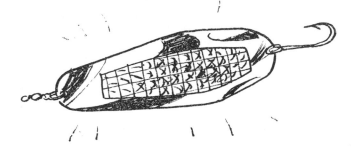

purple — you name it! As a consequence, many lures now have a reflective tape imbedded in clear plastic which flashes back the same dazzling array.

You can even buy this tape for application to your own favorite lure. One local expert adds reflective tape to his Strip-Teasers (Herring-Aid in the U.S.) and his Buzz-Bombs with considerable success. Maybe these reflecting lures, which break white light into its component colors, give the salmon a flash of the color it is seeking. Don't, however, add too much reflective tape. Our underwater camera tests show that a lure completely covered with reflective tape tended to inhibit strikes.

When we go down deep with our lures, we must remember that some portions of the color spectrum cannot penetrate very far under water.

```
15    RED
30
45          FLUOR-
            ESCENT    ORANGE
60
75
90                              YELLOW
105                                GREEN
120
135
150   DEPTHS OF                              BLUE
165   COLOR
      VISIBILITY
180
FEET
```

Deep Color Sensing

Despite the scientific facts about the fade-out of colors at depth, commercial trollers off the west coast of Vancouver Island are discovering apparently contradictory information. In their continuing search for salmon, they are trolling deeper and deeper and moving out to the very edge of the continental shelf. They are finding large chinooks at 600 feet or more. More surprising, these fish have definite color preferences.

At 600 feet there is no visible light of any kind. Yet the big chinooks can seemingly distinguish color. It seems to defy all logic, but the commercial trollers insist that salmon can choose between colors even at these great depths.

"HOT" LURES

Why does one lure consistently out-fish other apparently identical lures? Journeymen anglers have experienced this phenomenon many times. While they can't give any conclusive reasons why one is better than another, they know that such fish producers are to be guarded with special care.

All good bucktailers have "hot" flies which out-produce all

others in their tackle box. Some minor nuance in color, shape, or action seems to really trigger those strikes. Certain of my plastic Strip Teaser bait holders give some extra little kick or flip to the herring. While I usually can't see any difference, the fish sure must!

The same phenomenon runs through the whole gamut of fishing. Certain plugs, spoons, flashtails, or hoochies have that special fish catching ingredient. Even dodgers, flashers, and diving planers seem to develop different fish attracting characteristics from their seemingly identical cousins. I haven't noticed any tendency for one downrigger to outfish another, but I'm keeping records.

When you get a lure which has these extraordinary properties,

study it in action next to the boat to see if anything looks different. If you notice something, try to get other similar lures to do the same thing — or at least watch for the special difference in each new one that you try.

Take pains to keep from losing these treasures. Don't use them when fishing right on the bottom or when trolling close to kelp beds where they might hang up and break off. If you get into a school of dogfish, take off your hot lures before the razor jaws do it for you.

SNAP!

Be very careful when using them in fast tides or in unfamiliar water where you can be swept into foul ground without warning.

Hot Lure Temptations

My own problem with hot lures is the temptation to use them when fishing with novices. I take out many business associates and out-of-

town visitors who aren't skilled in the use of my single action "knuckle-duster" reels, to me the best reels for sporting action and fun fishing.

But since I'm really keen to have my guest catch a good salmon, out go the hot lures. When they do their job and the reel screams its delightful fish-on message, I shout my usual, "Let him run!"

More often than I care to remember my excited guest can't wait to start winding in and jams his hand into the whirling reel handles.

The reel stops abruptly, the angler shouts (or curses) in pain, and the knuckle duster claims another victim. The sudden stop often pops the line and a lovely salmon swims away with my precious lure. Al-

though I try to use unproven lures with my fishing students and most guests, it's very hard to keep the hot ones in the tackle box.

KNOTS

There are a number of knots used in fishing, but the most popular on monofilament line is the jam, or cinch, knot. Over 90 per cent of all knots tied in monofilament are of this type. It is ideal for tying

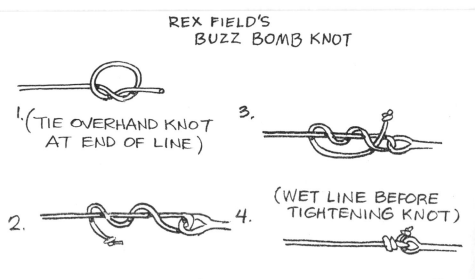

REX FIELD'S
BUZZ BOMB KNOT

1. (TIE OVERHAND KNOT AT END OF LINE)

2.

3.

4. (WET LINE BEFORE TIGHTENING KNOT)

lure to line, line to swivel, flasher to line, etc. Rhys Davis, inventor of the famous Strip Teaser lures, recently did some experiments with this widely used knot. There are a number of variations used by salmon anglers and Rhys tested their relative strength. He was amazed to discover that one version of the knot was far stronger than the

A.

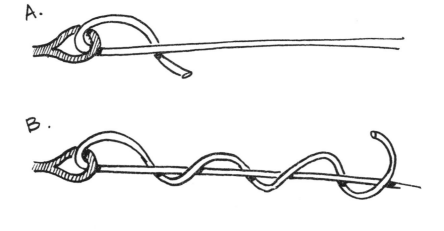

B.

NOTE: WET LINE
TO HELP IT SLIDE. PULL

NOTE:--
NOT THRU
EYE
C. EYE

PULL

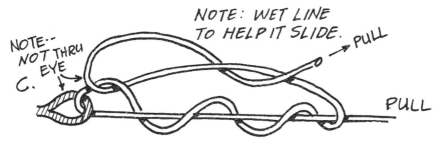

WITH KNOT THIS FAR ALONG, BEGIN TUGGING AT MAIN LINE, THEN END OF LINE. SLIDE LOOPS TOWARD EYE AS YOU PULL KNOT SNUG.

TIP: WHEN TYING LINE TO A *HOOK*, YOU CAN HOOK IT TO SOMETHING, TO GIVE YOU BOTH HANDS FREE TO WORK WITH KNOT.

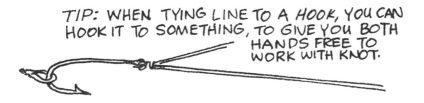

others. Some very minor variations were sometimes only half the strength of the proper knot.

CATCHING SMALL FISH

If you start catching small fish and others are catching large ones, it doesn't necessarily mean you are doing anything wrong. The fact

that you are getting strikes means that your gear is working satisfactorily.

It may be just the luck of the draw. I once hooked a doubleheader off Sidney using two similar lures at similar depths. One was a seven-pound coho and the other was a 36-pound chinook. Surely it was pure chance as to which fish took which bait. The salmon, however, may be segregated in schools of different sizes. The larger fish are often somewhat deeper than the little fellows. The school of big fish may also be highly localized in one hole or backeddy.

Another reason for catching small fish is the size of bait. Fisheries Department studies have definitely indicated that larger lures, on average, will catch larger fish. However, you can still catch small fish on big baits. I've had 10-inch grilse attack seven-inch herring, one right after the other, until I gave up and moved elsewhere.

RELEASING SMALL FISH

Legal size limits and the interests of conservation require that small salmon be returned to the water — unharmed if possible. But returning a fish is not always easy, and is sometime impossible if the

hooks are deeply imbedded in the eye, gill or other vital spot.

Many fishermen deplore the waste in throwing back a dying fish for the gulls or dogfish to eat when it could make a nice meal for the angler. Fisheries Department officials claim that any meaningful enforcement would be impossible if mortally wounded fish were exempt from the regulations. Unscrupulous anglers would merely jam the hooks into the gills of any undersized fish and toss it into the fish box. Even law abiding sportsmen would have a difficult time determining when a fish was too badly hurt to survive.

All undersized fish must be released — and as gently as possible. I learned in my Fish Commission days, and again at the Undersea Gardens, that handling fish improperly causes serious damage.

Holding a salmon with dry hands removes the protective slime from its body and fungus infections usually result. We used to be amazed to watch an apparently vigorous salmon released into the Undersea Gardens become covered with fungus growth and die within a week or two because some of its protective slime had been removed in handling.

Using wet hands is much better, but makes the fish as slippery as a cake of soap. As a result, you either squeeze so hard that the internal organs may be damaged or the fish keeps slipping onto the deck, rubbing off slime and often doing other damage.

I much prefer to unhook the fish without touching it at all. Don't

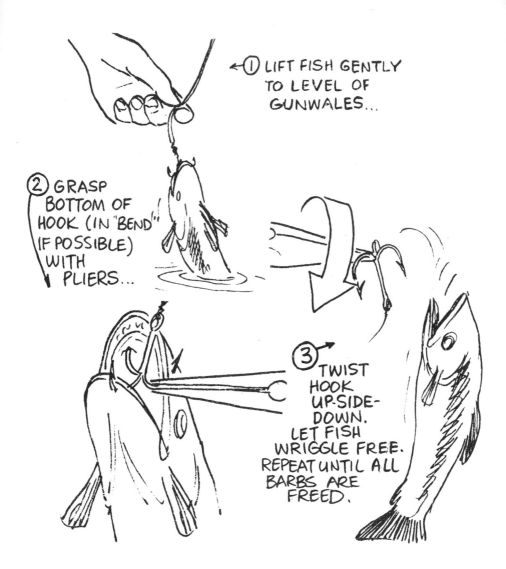

① LIFT FISH GENTLY TO LEVEL OF GUNWALES...

② GRASP BOTTOM OF HOOK (IN "BEND" IF POSSIBLE) WITH PLIERS...

③ TWIST HOOK UP-SIDE-DOWN. LET FISH WRIGGLE FREE. REPEAT UNTIL ALL BARBS ARE FREED.

use a landing net, which will knock off scales and slime, but just lift the line up to the gunwale of the boat. Grasp the hook in the bend, if possible, with a pair of long-nosed pliers. Turn the hook upside down (with the point downward) and let the fish wiggle free.

The salmon will usually give a couple of thrashing flips and the hook will pop loose. He will fall into the water without having been touched by hand or net. This system works well, even on fish hooked with two or three barbs of a treble hook. When you first grasp the hook with the pliers, one of the trebles often comes free, and the other, when you turn the hook over.

Washington Department of Fisheries claim that scale loss is the greatest source of mortality among small salmon caught and released. Removal of scales allows water to be drawn out through the skin, dehydrating the fish. Scale loss of 25 per cent can be fatal.

They recommend a special hook releaser which can be made easily from a coat hanger. This method can't save a salmon hooked

deep in the throat or gills, but if you use good sized hooks they can't swallow them as easily. Carefully releasing small salmon will provide more large ones for better fishing next year.

However, major increases in minimum size limits in British Columbia, Washington, Oregon and elsewhere have added a whole new dimension to the problem of releasing fish. As this edition goes to press minimum size limits for chinook are over 24 inches in some areas. This size is upwards of a 5-pound fish, a trophy for many fresh-water species.

Releasing fish this size raises several issues — physical, logistics, and conservation. Handling it without scale loss or injury can be very difficult. Using a net will almost certainly result in loss of both scales and protective mucous. Just lifting the fish out of the water by the hook can cause tearing and internal damage.

Most anglers, eager to keep a fine meal, will bring the fish aboard and hold it firmly down on the deck while measuring to see if it is legal. Then it is lifted back over the side for release. In my opinion, all this handling is usually fatal, even with careful and ex-

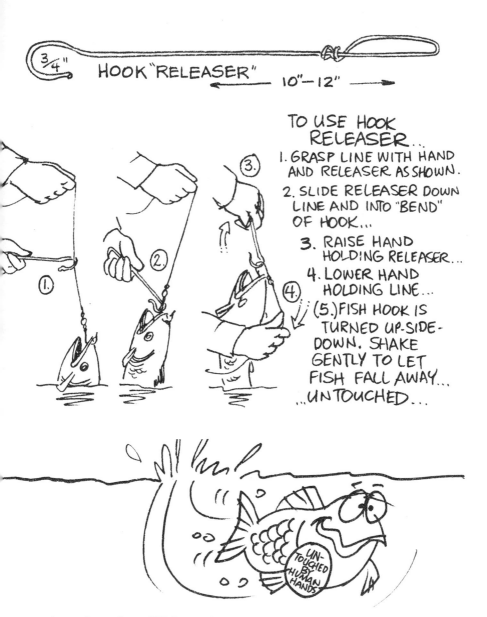

HOOK "RELEASER" ← 10"–12" →

3/4"

TO USE HOOK
   RELEASER...
1. GRASP LINE WITH HAND
   AND RELEASER AS SHOWN.
2. SLIDE RELEASER DOWN
   LINE AND INTO "BEND"
   OF HOOK...
3. RAISE HAND
   HOLDING RELEASER...
4. LOWER HAND
   HOLDING LINE...
(5.) FISH HOOK IS
   TURNED UP-SIDE-
   DOWN. SHAKE
   GENTLY TO LET
   FISH FALL AWAY...
   ...UNTOUCHED...

UN-
TOUCHED
BY
HUMAN
HANDS

perienced anglers. With novices, it is almost certainly a death sentence.

I don't see how such size limits help to preserve our salmon runs. An angler may catch five or six undersized fish before he gets one or two he can keep. Rather than release five or six fish to die, why not let him keep his first two smaller ones and save the others?

Fisheries Department officials have shown me studies purported to show that released fish do survive. These tests, on a commercial

48

troller, considered that a fish survived if it lived four hours in a tank on deck. Even then, there was significant mortality. Show me some two- or three-week survival data and I'll support their position.

I still believe the best method to preserve our salmon runs is to move the commercial seines and gillnets to the mouths of the spawning rivers. This "terminal fishery" would allow each river system to be managed individually, allowing sufficient escapement for spawning, then harvesting the rest.

The present method of fishing in the ocean and corridors (Juan de Fuca and Johnstone Straits) is a form of Russian Roulette. Commercial nets fish intermingling stocks, catching salmon from abundant river stocks as well as those which are almost wiped out. River-mouth harvest can mean better fishery management.

Commercial interests claim that river-mouth fish are of lower quality, but market prices of most river-mouth fish are just as high as ocean caught specimens.

If fisheries authorities insist on further restrictions on sport anglers who catch less than 10 per cent of the fish, they might consider barbless hooks instead of large size limits.

FISHING DIARY

When I worked as a biologist for the Oregon Fish Commission in my younger days, I was impressed with the mounting evidence that salmon migrations followed a rigid schedule. The Commissioners discovered that the Willamette River fall chinook run, for example, arrived at the mouth of the Columbia River on almost the same date each summer.

YOU WILL RETURN TO THIS SPOT... EXACTLY... IN PRECISELY ONE YEAR.

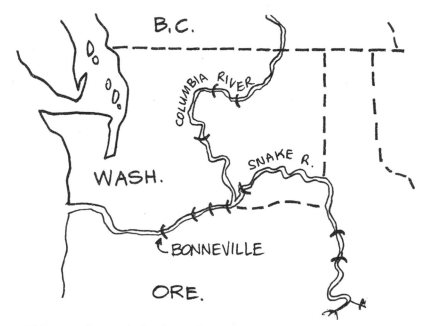

This was the period when all the huge hydro-electric dams were being built along the Columbia. Although Bonneville Dam had been in operation for many years, most of the others were just in the final planning or early construction stages. Data from the salmon migrations over the Bonneville Fish Ladders showed the big runs bound for the Snake River and the Upper Columbia arrived on schedule each year. If the fish were 24 to 48 hours late, the senior biologists were very concerned. It usually indicated that something drastic had happened, often a severe drop-off in the whole run to that particular river.

As each additional dam was built, the biologists learned that the fish could find their way over the dam all right, but each one delayed the salmon by an average of a day and a half. As more of the concrete barriers went up, the cumulative delays were too much for the salmon's delicate biological clock. They just couldn't make it to the spawning ground, and these magnificent upper river runs were wiped out or severely curtailed.

Migration patterns follow a regular schedule, not only at spawning time, but throughout the life cycle of the salmon. Each species, and each individual river strain, seems to have its own pre-programmed schedule of activity. Just as the swallows return to Capistrano each year on almost the identical date, a specific run of salmon will arrive in the same area at the same time each year.

For this reason, many high liners, or top rods, keep a diary on each fish they catch. After a while a pattern emerges for the various salmon fishing spots. My own diaries soon tipped me off to a concentration of small cohos which arrive off Yarrow Point near my home in early May. I can now list dozens of runs of cohos and chinooks which show up like clockwork each year within five miles of my front door. (A suggested *Fishing Diary* begins on page 180.)

These records can tell you a lot more than just the date each salmon arrives. If you tabulate such facts as depth, time of day and what the tide was doing, you will have more fish habit information to guide you. It is also very important to record detailed facts on the lure, its color, size, action — fast spin, slow wobble, etc. — information on flashers, leader length, and similar data.

I have found this type of diary extremely valuable in fly fishing. Color preferences seem to repeat themselves and trolling speeds have an annual pattern. Some runs of Cowichan Bay cohos, for instance, strike most readily at very fast, almost planing speeds.

A big school of cohos which arrives at Cherry Point about September 15 often won't take a fly unless it is 150 feet or more behind the boat. We discovered this preference one day when one boat took three cohos while 30 others got nothing. We asked all the usual questions of the successful angler, and we seemed to be doing everything he was. When we finally asked how much line he had out, he startled us by saying, "One hundred and fifty feet." When we lengthened our lines from the usual 40 to 75 feet, we hooked a beauty within a few minutes.

This preference for a long line defies a logical explanation, since the fly stays near the surface no matter how much line you let out. It works this way every year, however, and the long line seems the key factor.

This example shows that your diary should include data on what happens to other boats in the area. If other boats are having success, we record as many facts about it as we can. Some of my best diary information was picked up from other boats on days when I was skunked. This information is usually about some lure or technique I don't often use. The diary is a constant reminder to keep myself flexible and to try new methods if my regular procedure doesn't produce fish.

I keep a large notebook with a page for each day, from May through October, and one page for each winter week, when I don't fish as often. Another method is to keep each trip on a separate sheet of paper. Twelve manila folders or envelopes are marked with the months and the individual diary sheets are placed in the proper month. This system is very simple and will work well for a number of years. You just take the current month's folder with you on each trip.

DOGFISH

These local sharks are a terrible nuisance and can bite off a lot of expensive tackle. Their only saving grace is the thrill they can give a

child or novice fisherman if nothing else is biting. When I was operating as a charter guide, dogfish brightened several very dull trips. When I saw the telltale strike of the dogfish I would yell, "Shark! Shark!" and run around the boat with a worried look on my face.

After carefully sharpening my gaff, I would warn my charter guests to stand clear while I gaffed the shark and swung him up on the gunwale. Then I would show the razor-sharp teeth and wicked spikes behind the fins. My guests, especially those from inland areas, were fascinated.

One group became excited and wanted to keep the dogfish. I put it into the fish box and went on trolling. Some of my local friends trolled by and asked if we had any luck. My guests proudly held up the dogfish while my friends doubled up with laughter. "Private joke," I muttered darkly when my guests asked me what was so funny.

If you catch a dogfish, it does not mean there are no salmon. Both salmon and dogfish (and ling cod and sea birds) are often competing for the same food. It is just a matter of catching the salmon instead of the dogfish.

There are two basic techniques used to avoid dogfish:

1: **Troll faster.** All sharks have underslung jaws and roll over al-

most on their back to attack their prey. This somewhat clumsy action makes it more difficult for them to catch a fast moving lure.

2: **Use artificial lures.** Dogfish have a highly developed sense of smell and seem to be more attracted to herring and other natural baits.

MARKING A LOCATION

Since fishermen work in a three dimensional medium, finding the proper depth is not the whole answer to locating salmon. If we carefully count the number of pulls of line we have out, or use depth recording downriggers, we should know within reason how deep our lines are running.

When we get a strike, we should try also to mark the spot where the fish took the lure.

Many cartoons and jokes have had fishermen marking an "X" on the water or on the back of the boat. But it's a serious problem if you

want to get back to the action as quickly as possible. As you play a salmon, your boat drifts. In some strong tidal currents or brisk winds, you might be carried a mile or more before landing your salmon. If you don't mark the spot, you'll have a difficult time finding the fish again.

Inexperienced boatmen often think they have fixed their position by a simple reference to a single object on shore. They will say, "We were just opposite that red building (or the small hill with the rounded peak, etc.) when the fish hit." They forget that it is very difficult to know when you are exactly at right angles to a land mark. An error of 10 degrees in either direction is very common.

If you are even one-half mile from your marker, a 20 degree (10

...AND THERE'S A WHOLE SCHOOL OF 'EM BACK THERE -- JUST OFF FROM WHERE TH' EAGLE IS PERCHED IN TH' TREE!

on either side of a right angle) variation means that you can be 450 feet or more away from your intended position. If you are a mile away, you can be more than 900 feet from the last known position of the fish. If you are fishing off the open coast, you might be miles from any shore markings and the potential error becomes horrendous.

This arithmetic takes into account only the error in angle. It doesn't even consider the problem of measuring how far you are from that marker. You might be hundreds of feet nearer to or farther from the marker than when you first made your observation.

Range Markers
The only accurate method to determine your location on water is by

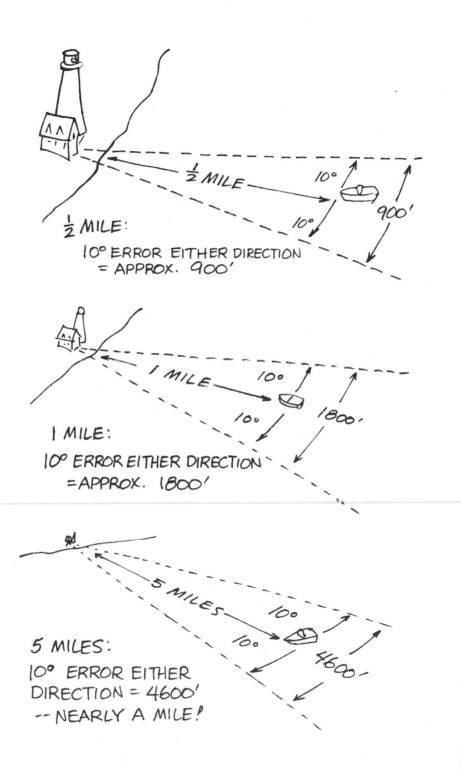

½ MILE:
10° ERROR EITHER DIRECTION
= APPROX. 900'

1 MILE:
10° ERROR EITHER DIRECTION
= APPROX. 1800'

5 MILES:
10° ERROR EITHER
DIRECTION = 4600'
-- NEARLY A MILE!

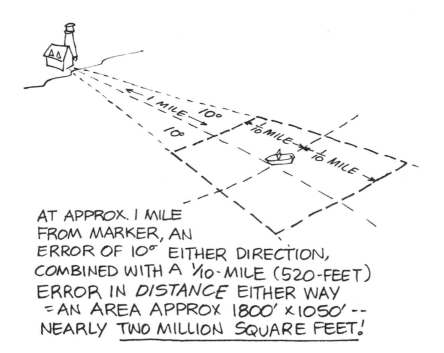

AT APPROX. 1 MILE
FROM MARKER, AN
ERROR OF 10° EITHER DIRECTION,
COMBINED WITH A 1/10-MILE (520-FEET)
ERROR IN *DISTANCE* EITHER WAY
= AN AREA APPROX 1800' x 1050' --
NEARLY TWO MILLION SQUARE FEET!

using the range marker, or "gunsight," method. This term simply means that you use two fixed objects, one lined up behind the other, to establish an exact line. The two objects shouldn't be too close together if you want pinpoint accuracy.

Then find two more fixed objects, as near as possible to a right angle from the first two, to fix a second definitive line marker. The spot where the two lines cross is your exact position. If you line up your markers accurately, you can establish your location with great precision. With a little practice, taking such markers becomes relatively easy.

In the excitement of a strike, especially the first strike of the day, it is difficult to remember to take range marks. Often we take our marks after we have been playing our fish for a minute or two. Then we should also note the direction of our drift. After landing the salmon, we return to our marked position and troll back against the direction of our earlier drift. This course should take us back over the original strike. You can also use this method to get an approximate fix on the location where a nearby boat hooked a fish.

Range markers are also a vital tool in deep fishing to keep you in water of the proper depth. You can fish along a set of markers to keep you from drifting into a reef or other foul ground. Many of the old pros use a complicated series of range markers to troll through twisting underwater canyons without mishap. (See page 60.)

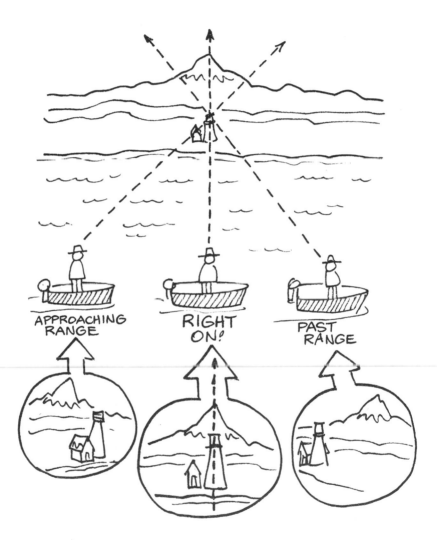

APPROACHING
RANGE

RIGHT
ON!

PAST
RANGE

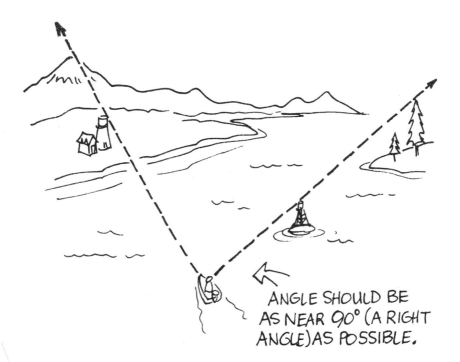

ANGLE SHOULD BE
AS NEAR 90° (A RIGHT
ANGLE) AS POSSIBLE.

These methods are especially effective for chinooks which tend to hang around a specific bottom feature or location. Cohos, which tend to move more actively, are sometimes difficult to pin down by

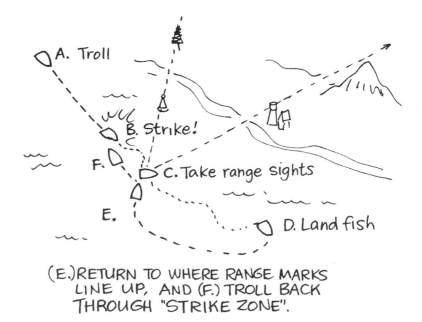

A. Troll

B. Strike!

F.

C. Take range sights

E.

D. Land fish

(E.) RETURN TO WHERE RANGE MARKS
LINE UP, AND (F.) TROLL BACK
THROUGH "STRIKE ZONE".

(REEF)

range markers. They often move with the tide, follow tide lines, or drifting schools of bait.

Floating Markers
In these open water situations, many experienced anglers throw over the side a floating object which tends to drift with the feeding

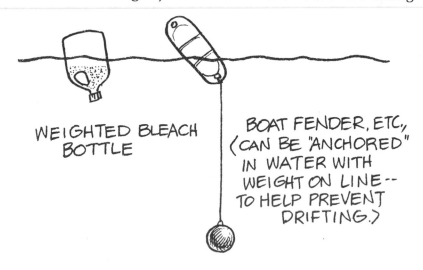

WEIGHTED BLEACH
BOTTLE

BOAT FENDER, ETC.,
(CAN BE "ANCHORED"
IN WATER WITH
WEIGHT ON LINE --
TO HELP PREVENT
DRIFTING.)

TO SIMPLIFY RETURNING
TO A SPOT BY USING RANGE
MARKERS...

...LINE UP ONE SET OF
MARKERS, THEN PROCEED
ALONG THIS LINE...

...UNTIL THE SECOND SET
OF MARKERS LINES UP.

fish. Commercial guides often have a special buoy for this purpose, but any floating object will do — a seat cushion, plastic bottle, even a piece of driftwood. Be sure to retrieve whatever you use before leaving the area to prevent littering.

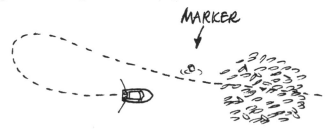

A point to remember is that cohos tend to remain in tight schools in the same manner as herring, candlefish, and other smaller fish. Often these coho schools are no more than 50 feet across, so you have to get to a fairly exact position to catch them. The fish may move away from your floating marker, but at least you have a starting point for your search. If you find the cohos again, you can always toss over another buoy.

TROLLING TIPS

When trolling across the current and making a turn, it is usually better to turn into the tide, rather than with the flow. This is especially important if you get a strike, but don't hook the fish. You want to get back to the same spot quickly.

Turning into the tidal flow will help you hold position. Turning with the current will allow the boat to be carried a long way down tide. It takes considerable time to work back up against the tide to your original position.

If I am forced to turn with the tide by other boats, reefs, or wind, I will sometimes pull up my gear and run back to the desired spot.

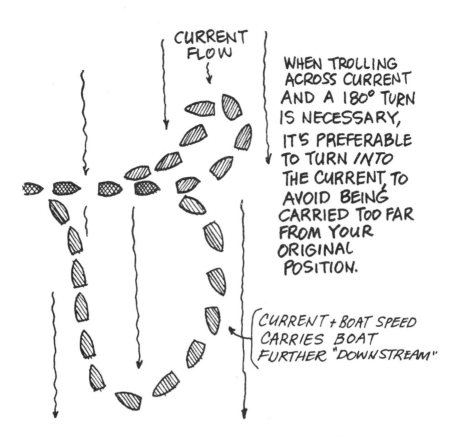

CURRENT FLOW

WHEN TROLLING ACROSS CURRENT AND A 180° TURN IS NECESSARY, IT'S PREFERABLE TO TURN *INTO* THE CURRENT, TO AVOID BEING CARRIED TOO FAR FROM YOUR ORIGINAL POSITION.

(CURRENT + BOAT SPEED CARRIES BOAT FURTHER "DOWNSTREAM")

This action is better than spending 15 minutes to half an hour working back through unproductive waters.

Try New Area

If you see no signs indicating the presence of salmon — birds, jumping fish, bait fish, or other boats catching fish — it is a good idea to keep moving into new water. Working the same water over and over is often less productive than moving to fresh, untried areas.

My own theory is that chinooks are somewhat territorial and move quickly to investigate anything new appearing in their area. When fishing winter chinooks particularly, I find that strikes come mostly on the first run through the fishing hole.

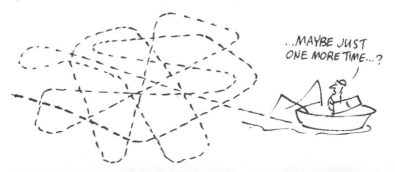

...MAYBE JUST ONE MORE TIME...?

DEPENDING UPON THE SIZE OF THE BOAT, YOU CAN TROLL TWO, THREE OR EVEN FOUR RODS, SUCCESSFULLY.

TWO ROD RIG

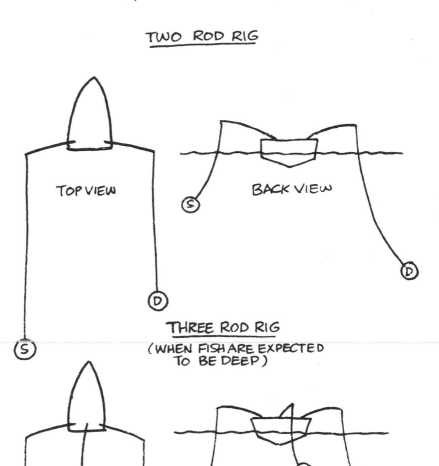

TOP VIEW

BACK VIEW

THREE ROD RIG
(WHEN FISH ARE EXPECTED TO BE DEEP)

(NOT AT EXACTLY SAME DEPTH)

ALTERNATE
FOUR-ROD RIG

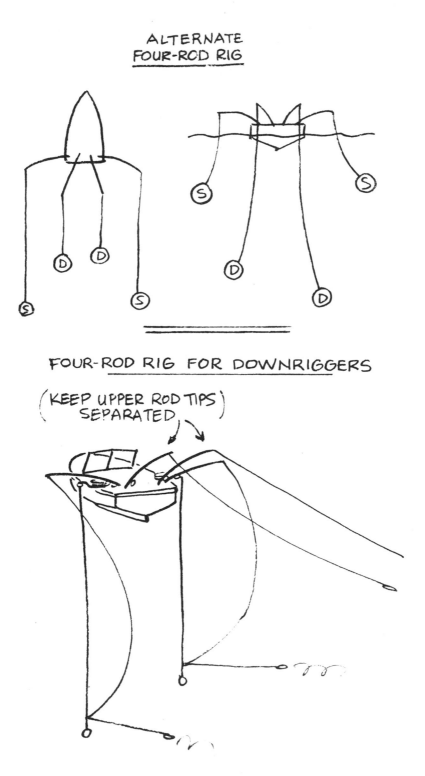

FOUR-ROD RIG FOR DOWNRIGGERS

(KEEP UPPER ROD TIPS
SEPARATED)

ALTERNATE
THREE-ROD RIG
(IF FISH ARE EXPECTED TO BE SHALLOW)

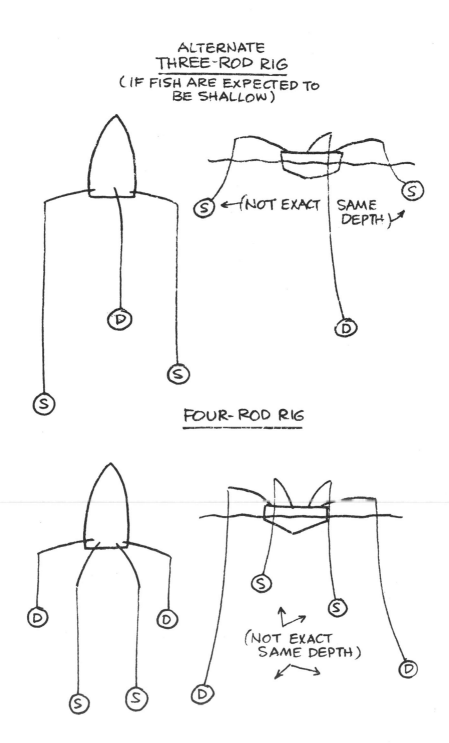

FOUR-ROD RIG

CHAPTER TWO By Charlie White

Trolling With Bait

Strip Teasers

Using natural bait is probably the most productive method of trolling if fishing derby records are any indication. Fisheries Department statistics for special permit areas in British Columbia support this view.

On Vancouver Island, the season-long King Fisherman contest — now discontinued — revealed that herring baits caught more fish and produced more prize winners than all other lures combined. Far and away the most popular method of rigging those baits in Canada is with the plastic-headed Strip Teaser (Herring-Aid in the U.S.). This curved bait holder helps give the herring or strip an erratic rolling

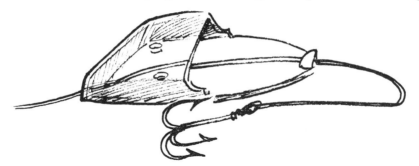

action which triggers lots of strikes.

Have you ever watched a school of herring, especially when predators are attacking? You'll notice that stunned or wounded herring behave in a characteristic manner. They appear to lose their stability and start twisting and rolling as they attempt to swim away. If they are badly wounded, they roll over and over in a gasping, jerky action. This is the type of behavior that excites predators to strike.

I learned my salmon fishing fundamentals with the Strip Teaser and went out on many trips with its inventor, Rhys Davis. The most popular models are the large Strip Teaser and the Super Strip Teaser (which hold herring strip) and the Minnow Teaser and Super Min-

"SUPER" TEASERS -- SLOW, LOOPING, CLOCKWISE ACTION.

now Teaser. The Super models cause the bait to turn clockwise in a slow looping circle. The regular models roll the bait in fast, tight counter-clockwise turns.

REGULAR/LARGE TEASERS -- FAST, TIGHT, COUNTER-CLOCKWISE ACTION.

These differences are important, especially when fishing without flashers or dodgers. The faster turning, regular Strip Teasers work well at the slow trolling speeds normally used for chinooks. The slower turning Super Strip Teasers often won't roll at all with the boat moving very slowly. For faster trolling, however, the Supers come alive. The bait leaps in an erratic "gasping" action as it flips over. This faster speed is excellent for cohos and also helps to keep away from the dogfish. The regular Teaser tends to spin like a dervish at a fast troll and is not as effective.

Bait action can be modified by adjusting the hooks. Pulling the hooks tight against the plastic head tends to speed up the action, while pulling them back toward the tail tends to slow down the roll. When trolling slowly with the regular Teaser, I even cock the hooks at an angle, tight against the plastic, to increase the roll and to give the bait a tantalizing side wobble. Rigging this way requires a good tight knot so the hook will hold at the angle you set it. I used to prefer treble hooks, and the illustrations in this book show them.

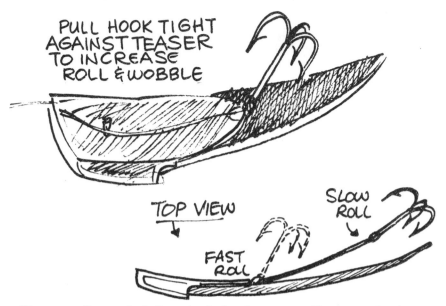

PULL HOOK TIGHT
AGAINST TEASER
TO INCREASE
ROLL & WOBBLE

TOP VIEW

FAST
ROLL

SLOW
ROLL

However, I now feel that single hooks are as effective in hooking a fish, and hold a fish more securely once hooked. They also are far less likely to injure undersized salmon. I still use trebles for whole herring since one hook is buried in the bait.

When fishing whole herring, I much prefer the Super models

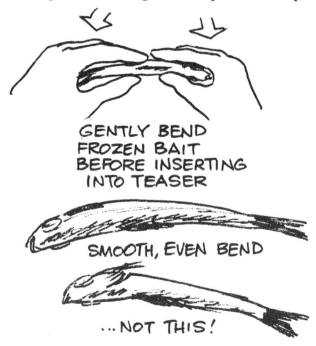

GENTLY BEND
FROZEN BAIT
BEFORE INSERTING
INTO TEASER

SMOOTH, EVEN BEND

...NOT THIS!

over the regular Teasers. The Super Minnow Teaser is used with four-and-one-half- to five-inch minnows and the Super Herring Teaser with seven-inch herring.

When fishing smaller minnows, I leave the hooks to hang free, but the frozen bait should be curved gently with the fingers before insertion in the Teaser. A nice even curve is desirable.

With larger herring, place one hook of the treble through the bait about one-half inch behind the dorsal fin and about one-third up the side from the vent. This position can be varied with different

HOOKUP FOR LARGER HERRING

•FOR SLOW SPIN AT SLOW TROLLING SPEED, PUT HOOK THROUGH
BAIT JUST ABOVE VENT. AND... USE SLIGHT TO MEDIUM BEND.

• FOR A FAST SPIN AT A
SLOW TROLL SPEED, PUT HOOK
ABOUT ⅔ DOWN, IN LINE WITH BACK OF DORSAL FIN, AND
USE A BIG BEND IN BAIT.

sized herring and to get other lure action. Pull the line up tight to give the desired curve to the bait after shaping it with your fingers. The greater the curve, the faster the roll of the bait.

Other Bait Holders

Other popular bait holders are Krippled Minnow, Krippled Herring, and Herring Magic. The Krippled Minnow rig provides a revolving action similar to the Strip Teaser lures and can be just as effective.

Herring Magic produces a very different action. Its shovel-nosed front causes the herring to swim through the water with a darting action. Faster trolling speeds accentuate this erratic swimming motion. There are times when salmon don't seem to like a rolling bait and Herring Magic or plugs may be effective at these times.

"HERRING MAGIC"

Rigging Herring

There are many ways to rig herring without the use of bait holders. The following diagrams illustrate a few of the popular methods:

1. THREAD BACK HOOK Ⓐ INTO MEMBRANE UNDER MOUTH -- OUT THROUGH TOP OF MOUTH. DO SAME WITH FRONT HOOK Ⓑ.

2. THEN PUT BACK HOOK Ⓐ THROUGH HERRING, IN TOP OF EYE SOCKET. DO THE SAME WITH FRONT HOOK Ⓑ.

TOP VIEW

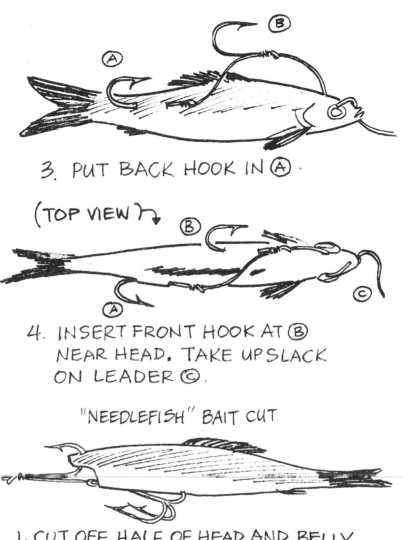

3. PUT BACK HOOK IN Ⓐ.

(TOP VIEW)

4. INSERT FRONT HOOK AT Ⓑ
NEAR HEAD. TAKE UP SLACK
ON LEADER Ⓒ.

"NEEDLEFISH" BAIT CUT

1. CUT OFF HALF OF HEAD AND BELLY.
REMOVE INTERNAL ORGANS, GILL
COVERS.

2. FRONT HOOK IS PUT THROUGH TOP
OF HEAD (FROM BELOW) TO HELP HOLD
BAIT IN VERTICAL POSITION.

3. ONE PRONG OF TREBLE HOOK IS PUT
INTO BACKBONE, FROM BELOW, AS SHOWN.

TROLLING WITH PLUG CUT FROZEN HERRING

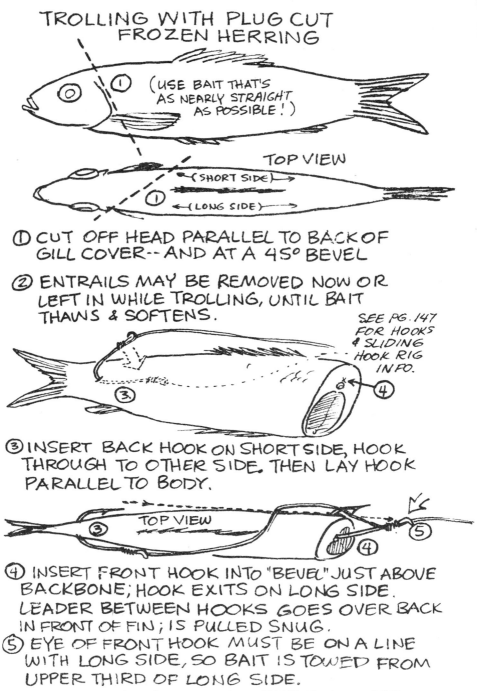

(USE BAIT THAT'S AS NEARLY STRAIGHT AS POSSIBLE!)

TOP VIEW

←(SHORT SIDE)→

←(LONG SIDE)→

① CUT OFF HEAD PARALLEL TO BACK OF GILL COVER -- AND AT A 45° BEVEL

② ENTRAILS MAY BE REMOVED NOW OR LEFT IN WHILE TROLLING, UNTIL BAIT THAWS & SOFTENS.

SEE PG. 147 FOR HOOKS & SLIDING HOOK RIG INFO.

③ INSERT BACK HOOK ON SHORT SIDE, HOOK THROUGH TO OTHER SIDE. THEN LAY HOOK PARALLEL TO BODY.

TOP VIEW

④ INSERT FRONT HOOK INTO "BEVEL" JUST ABOVE BACKBONE; HOOK EXITS ON LONG SIDE. LEADER BETWEEN HOOKS GOES OVER BACK IN FRONT OF FIN; IS PULLED SNUG.

⑤ EYE OF FRONT HOOK MUST BE ON A LINE WITH LONG SIDE, SO BAIT IS TOWED FROM UPPER THIRD OF LONG SIDE.

▶ TROLLED *VERY SLOWLY*, THIS RIG GIVES BAIT A LARGE, SLOW ROLL.

CHAPTER THREE   By Lee Straight

Lee Straight for 33 years was Outdoor Editor of the Vancouver Sun *and is one of Canada's top outdoorsmen. He is an acknowledged authority on both salt-water and fresh-water angling, and author of Heritage House book,* How to Catch Trout.

Plug and Spoon Techniques

Among the most neglected lures in salmon sport fishing are the "hardware" lures — spoon and plug, trolled alone, not in a combination with a flasher or dodger. There are times and places when a lone plug or spoon is most deadly, whether fishing the sea, lake or river.

Plugs and spoons are at their best in clear salmon waters when fish are plentiful. They are easy to keep in action. No bait to cut beforehand, or to be torn, leaving you dragging an improperly baited hook for some time before checked. Hardware lures are, except when fouled with seaweed, working all the time. A good hardware man will outfish the bait man every time when the fish are on the prod and plentiful. Proof of that is in the commercial troller's gear. The commercial man seldom bothers with live or cut bait. Instead he concentrates on searching out the fish, getting down to them, then keeping his lures in action.

In addition to experimenting with depths, discussed elsewhere in this book and mentioned in most other salmon fishing books, the expert spoon and plug fisherman experiments with speed, color or shape, and the distance behind the sinker.

In clear winter-time waters, with herring spawning in some harbors near eel grass or wharf piling, the appropriate-sized spoon will often outfish live bait. I've seen a spoon snapped up by salmon when they were feeding, not on herring which were all about, but on tiny euphausid shrimps. I suppose they strike a spoon or small plug in competition, since the salmon and the swarming small fish — anchovies, herring, shiners and smelt — are all feeding on the clouds of tiny shrimp.

Plug and Spoon Basics
Some basic rules of spoon and plug fishing:

Keep hooks sharp. If rusty, touch up the entire outer bend of the

hook for easy sinking into flesh.

Use spoons or plugs alone when possible in clear waters — more fun, easier to keep in action, often taken more eagerly.

Start without a sinker, then add gradually heavier sinkers, of the slip variety, until you find the feeding level.

SPOONS

On spoons, use the long-pointed single hooks preferred by commercial fishermen. They hold fish better than multiple-pointed hooks and, if hung right, hook fish just as quickly. By hung right I mean having single hooks swimming point-up behind the spoon. Spoons usually swim in a sled-fashion with the convex, or bulbous side of the rear end, towards the sea-floor. If the single hook is clenched into

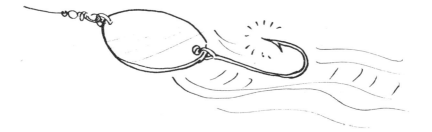

the rear eye or split ring so that it rides point-up it catches far less weed and just as many salmon.

Abalone (pearl) types of spoon usually outdraw all others. Next most effective, on the average, are those of chrome or nickel with many dimples. The overlays of stick-on Prism-Lite paper, sold in packages, certainly dress up a spoon.

Many anglers like to try half-and-half, brass-nickel or copper-nickel, or painted red-white spoons. I haven't satisfied myself that they are ever better than chrome but do know they're often worse. In addition, chrome is far easier to keep bright than the cheaper nickel plate.

Thin spoons are more lively for trolling. The heavy-bladed are for casting. The spinning variety of spoon, as opposed to the wobbling variety, exerts much drag. I use spinners only in conjunction with trolled streamer flies or, occasionally, as a casting lure for estuary coho fishing in fall, or in rivers.

Length of line between weight and spoon is not nearly so important as with plugs. Spoons have their own action, an erratic, tanta-

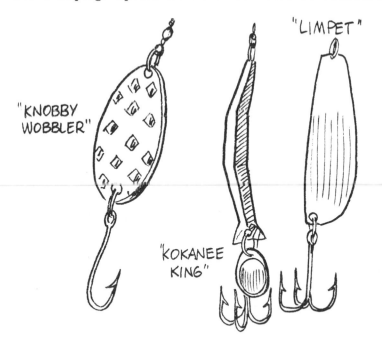

lizing, wobbling swim, unless trolled so fast they spin. I find them less effective when trolled that fast.

Some thin-bladed spoons I like are the Kokanee Killer, Kokanee King, Limpet, Tom Mack, Gibbs Stewart, Gibbs Diamond, Knobby Wobbler, Skinny Minny, McMahon, Canadian Wonder and any of their copies.

The abalone shell spoons and spinners I've found excellent, the spinners being supplied without hooks for fastening ahead of trolled streamer flies. The wobbling spoons are rigged with an excellent single hook. There are some imitation abalone lures of plastic.

For doubling as casting lures, though less lively when retrieved, the heavy-bladed wobbling spoons are preferable and can be used for trolling. Some suggested patterns are Krocodile, either Swedish or locally made, Needlefish, Tempter, Dardevl, Fat Max, 88, Candlefish, Kitamat and Hotrod.

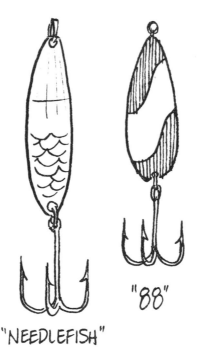

"88"

"NEEDLEFISH"

The various heavy-bladed, shaft-weighted spinners like the Metric, Super Metric, Sneak and (golf)Tee Spoons are old favorites.

PLUGS

Plugs are more sensitive to varying speeds. They have two basic actions — the tail-waggle and the dart from side to side. Tyee trollers, working the sea pools at the mouths of rivers to which these large, almost mature chinook salmon are homing, find them provoked best by slow-travelling, waggly lures. They troll so slowly the plugs seldom dart much from side to side, but they waggle. This waggle is so important that much attention is paid to a good "hinge" at the leader connecting point.

If the plug has a hole through it, with a harness made up of nose swivel, nylon string, and one or two treble hooks, the nose swivel should protrude from the hole in the plug body so its front ring is right at the lip. A heavy nylon monofilament or wire leader, run

NOSE SWIVEL (OR BEAD CHAIN) MUST ALLOW FREE HINGE ACTION HERE

straight into the hole in the plug, to one or more hooks, may severely inhibit that waggling action.

Darting Plug

Sometimes a fast-trolled, darting plug is more productive. The same plugs will work for both speeds of trolling, but at higher speed some dart violently from side to side, so widely at times that it may foul another line trolled from the same boat. The "cup-faced" plugs like the old Lucky Louie, Rex Field, Hi-Liner and other "rowboat" plugs, are good at low speed. Those with a "chin" protruding from the cupped front, dubbed "shovel-nose" by professional guides, work better at high speed and are sluggish at low speed.

Lazy, waggling plugs seem most effective trolled about 25 to 40 feet behind the sinker, with the sinker some 10 to 20 feet behind the

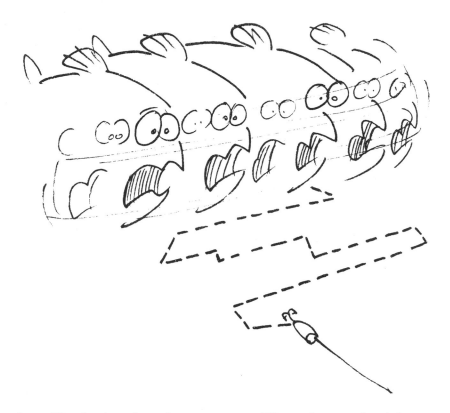

boat. The darting plugs dart even more if kept closer to the sinker, as close as six feet but usually about 12. Darting plugs are good, trolled deep on long 100-foot lines, for feeder chinooks; but on shorter lines, nearer the surface, for cohos. Large plugs select larger fish.

Leader thickness is more important in plug and spoon trolling than with dodgers and flashers. If you are trolling such light lures from limber rods, you can go down as low as 10-pound test for cohos and jack chinooks, and as low as 30-pound test with heavy, Tyee-type chinooks. Even 20-pound test isn't too thin with a limber rod and light sinker.

There seems less need for thin leaders with rapidly trolled lures,

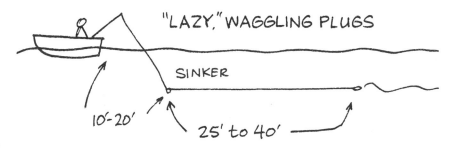

"LAZY," WAGGLING PLUGS

SINKER

10'-20'

25' to 40'

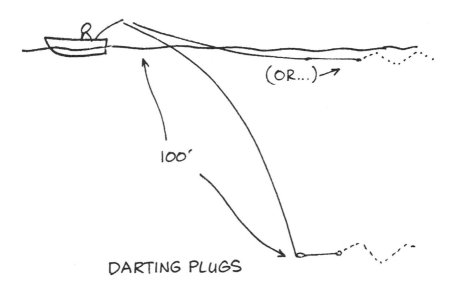

(OR...)➚

100'

DARTING PLUGS

but it must help. Experiments have proved beyond doubt that fish will take a lure more eagerly if the lure is by itself on a leader and if the leaders are thinner. Sometimes fish investigate knots ahead of the spoon but pass up the spoon itself.

Keep sinkers small and dark. Some anglers soak their new sinkers in sea water to turn them dark. Others paint their sinkers white, then blaze-orange, to attract fish (they believe). Some even

paint their boat propellers blaze-orange. I don't mind that idea, but I'd prefer to troll all plugs and spoons on unsinkered lines if I could get down to the fish that way.

Many anglers, including commercial fishermen, take pains to keep their own odor off the lures, soaking them in a bucket of fresh or sea water, or rubbing them with aniseed (licorice) oil. Some just scrub them with herring oil or against the flesh of another salmon. Many believe that some anglers smell less than others, thus accounting for the outstanding "fish sense" that some seem more blessed with than others. I doubt this theory. I believe that the more successful anglers are those who pay more attention to detail, watch for natural signs of feeding, and fish longer.

Questionable Method

I remember interviewing an old commercial troller about the subject of keeping human odor off lures. He said he combined the deodorizing process with a brightening safeguard by soaking his spoons. The moment they were lifted from the sea he dropped them in buckets of dilute copper sulphate solution. He said that it kept the brass lures bright, too.

I've long wondered about his conclusion, particularly since I've learned that copper sulphate ("bluestone") is deadly poison and, even in very dilute solution, repels fish. Octopus hunting scuba divers used to squirt it from ketchup and detergent dispenser bottles into the lairs of octopuses to drive them out.

I remain neutral by ignoring all rinsing or dousing techniques and it probably costs me some fish. One of my fishing acquaintances soaks his lures in detergent solution, particularly after using a polish such as Brasso. It's possible a lure is less offensive to a fish after the traces of Brasso are washed off, but I feel that it would become common practice if anyone had produced conclusive proof that it is effective. I say, forget it.

CHAPTER FOUR By Lee Straight

Dodger-Flasher Trolling

The most common error made by trollers of flashers, surprisingly slow to be appreciated even by accomplished anglers, is too light a leader between the flasher and bait or lure.

That flasher-dodger blade has much resistance to side pull. When the fish strikes the bait or lure, it has good resistance against

the breadth of the blade. As a result, it can pop a surprisingly thick leader. Or, in attempting to flee, the fish has that great blade flapping at its tail. A good thrust easily snaps a thin leader.

Remember that a flasher or dodger is a moving lure. Subterfuge isn't nearly so important as with a still bait. I use no less than 30-pound test leaders with cohos or winter chinooks, preferably 40-pound with Tyees or when trolling in strong tides.

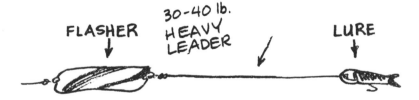

Some anglers go to the extreme of using surgical tubing shock-cords below or above their dodgers. That is just too bulky a leader. Fish have to be eager indeed to take a lure with one of those leaders between flasher and bait. It is not so critical when above the flasher. I've never had a salmon pop a leader since I went heavier, though it possibly has cost me in terms of fish hooked. I like shortish, 16- to 22-inch leaders for cohos; longish, 30- to 50-inches for chinooks. Likely it's because cohos will chase more readily and are provoked better by tantalizing action. I've never been able to interview the fish to find out why.

I avoid flashers, in contrast with dodgers. (A flasher is a rotation blade; the dodger is a zig-zagging or "swimming" blade.) One blade, however, can be made to serve both purposes by your speed

through the water and by the amount of curvature in the blade. The reason I dislike flashers is that they twist line, even the wire lines which I prefer for sea-trolling and which are far more productive.

But flashers often outfish dodgers, particularly at depth, as in winter trolling. I usually start with my dodgers swinging, then bend one into a flasher after lack of success. If it takes fish, then I may change both lines to flashers or just haul in the others and troll with one rod.

...ON THE OTHER HAND --
IF IT *DOES* CATCH FISH...

The speed of "dodge," or rotation, is increased by further kinking the bends at front or rear, not always easy in a sturdy blade. I usually slow the speed of rotation by adding more bend halfway down the blade, continuing the curve of the front kink. Bending the middle so that it continues the kink of the rear of the blade makes it swing or spin more.

Size of dodger-flasher seems more important in winter when you want fish to see it further at those murky depths. Only your tolerance of the hard-towing, heavy throbbing tackle limits the size of the blade. I dislike the commercial types but if meat is more important than the fun of playing a fish, then the largest blades are your best killers.

A good modification for dodgers is the addition of a brilliant stick-on sheet called Prism-Lite which looks like scaly fish hide, sold

in packages. I don't believe color matters much in dodgers, but brilliance in flashers must matter. These paste-ons flash brilliantly, look very fishy and are easily added. Try them.

Most trollers use too short a rod. They seem okay and are sold cheaply. I prefer rods of nine to 11 feet, stiff in the butt and just lively enough in the tip to show the pulsating action of the flasher. It must be strong enough to support over a pound of sinker and the

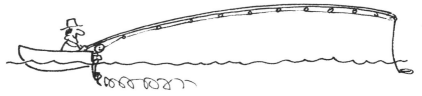

large flasher, or a hard-dragging planer. A bonus of long rods is that they keep lines spread better, almost a requirement in small, narrow boats.

If you use a single-action reel, which hangs below the rod handle, it should be located much nearer the rod butt than is preferred for

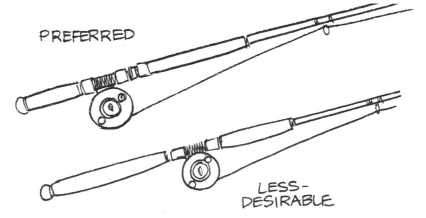

PREFERRED

LESS-
DESIRABLE

top-of-the-rod, star drag reels. It's a long reach on some boat rods otherwise. Few makers turn out rods with locking reel seats set low, but careful shopping will turn up some better than others.

The reason I prefer metal (monel) lines for trolling is that they stretch so little, hook fish more surely, telegraph flasher action to the rod tip, and jolt the angler much more when he is playing fish. Much more exciting! Just take care in storing it on the reel and don't let a wind blow you back onto such lines when you cut the motor to play a fish. They loop on themselves and can kink and break when again pulled tight.

I think the greatest problem the dodger-flasher troller faces is the speed of his boat. Most of us fish from powerboats. Few medium- to large-sized power boats will run less than three miles per hour. The beginner angler often has too much trouble keeping his speed low enough to handle flashers, let alone the even slower dodgers. He may be tempted to abandon that technique for trolling lone spoons or plugs, or just mooching, strip-casting or still-fishing with bait.

There is nothing wrong with these methods. I prefer them as being more sporting. But when you're coastal cruising and don't know the fish holes, or have guests who just can't be taught quickly

to stripcast or mooch, you do much better by trolling, searching out the fish.

The flasher-dodger outfits for trolling I prefer are two or three long, stiff, two-piece rods with 30-pound test monofil line, using chrome-plated commercial type flashers. Troll them as slow as you can travel without fouling your spark plugs, allowing them to rotate. Use a pair of good ballbearing swivels on each flasher, sprayed with oil between uses. I like heavy, firm herring strips or plug-cut herring — not light-cut or old — the strips preferably in Strip-Teaser holders. Add variety by using a spoon, hoochy type squid bait, or a streamer fly.

Two good rules of heavy trolling are to use strong line and, to avoid seaweed, closely trim all knots.

Many flasher anglers feel that a matched outfit is essential. Two Washington-Oregon authorities on that efficient kind of gear actually recommend makes and models of rod for the job — basically, seven to nine feet long with stiff butts but lively tips so you can see the rod throbbing to a spinning flasher as against merely a swinging (swimming) dodger. The big blades as mentioned earlier can be used as a dodger or flasher depending upon the action given them by varying speed through the water.

I've carefully studied the reports of those experts and see no evidence that they proved their favorite rods any more productive than longer rods or than those with more limber butt sections. The main requirement is a tip that is fairly sensitive but strong enough to withstand the tremendous strain of the towed, spinning flasher and sometimes large amounts of weight, or of a deep-diving planer.

I know some mighty productive B.C. chinook trollers whose Canadian versions of a matched outfit look totally unlike a Washingtonian's. They use a single-action reel mounted below the rod when being wound, closer to the butt than the multiplier jobs that Americans must mount atop the rod and further up the handle to keep reel handles from winding up their shirt fronts.

As for matching rod, flasher and lure, as some claim pays off, I suspect the tendency to be dogmatic. In a lifetime of fishing, I've not been able to discover angling techniques quite that conclusive. I eagerly await invitations to trips that will persuade me that I'm too sceptical, but I'm not holding my breath. I can just as easily point out other reasons for an efficient angler's success, forgotten by him out of modesty because he, like so many of us, enjoys theorizing.

Two of the greatest touchstones of angling success, even when merely trolling, are just doing it more than others and, while fishing, being more alert. It is just as important to stare balefully and diligently at the trolling rod tip as at the tip of the rod of the moocher's probing outfit.

Jigging-Driftfishing Lures

Buzz-Bombs

Jigging lures, or driftfishing lures, a name originated by Victoria outdoor columnist Alec Merriman and me when this type of salmon fishing first became popular in B.C., have been used all over the world for a hundred years or more. They first became popular in British Columbia in the 1960s when Rex Field invented the revolutionary "Buzz-Bomb." At about the same time, Wolfe Marine began importing a Norwegian jig called a Stingsilda for commercial fishermen. When the cod boats complained that the lures caught too many salmon which their licenses did not permit them to keep, enterprising owner John Wolfe introduced the lure to the sport fishing trade. (Jigging is not to be confused with snagging which is deliberately trying to impale a fish with the lure and which is illegal.)

Unlike trolling lures, these jigs work best when they are fluttering down on a slack line. This action simulates that of severely wounded baitfish which tend to drift down from the school. The Buzz-Bomb, along with my jigging lure design, adds a vibration to the lure to attract fish.

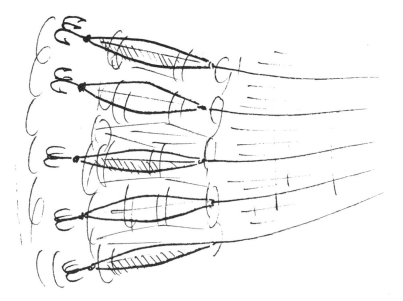

There is no doubt that certain vibrations in the water will attract fish. When I was a guide in the Underseas Gardens in Victoria, B.C., I remember a vivid example. A 10-pound chinook had just been added to the fish display and charged around frantically. It bumped its head sharply against a large rock and began to quiver and roll over in distress. It must have been putting out some sort of vibration

because many other fish in the area began to gather. Some even came from around a 90-degree corner, out of sight of the distressed salmon.

What makes the memory so vivid was the action that followed. A huge lingcod, estimated at more than 50 pounds, appeared out of nowhere and streaked for the salmon. We knew the ling had been on the other side of the exhibit where it had been lying quietly for days.

The vibrations of the distressed fish had awakened it and brought it from a distance of over 50 feet. The ling grabbed the salmon by the head and held on tight while it thrashed violently. As more than 50 spectators watched in awe, it worked its mouth farther along the salmon's body. Within a few minutes, the entire 10-pound salmon was in the ling's grotesquely distended stomach, only the corner of the tail visible in its jaw. The ling couldn't even lie flat on the bottom with her bulging gut, so she just tilted at an awkward angle and didn't move for another week!

Rex Field and his son, Doug, conducted some interesting tests to prove the sonic attraction properties of their Buzz-Bomb lure. In a quiet marina near their home in Courtenay, B.C., they dropped one near a school of small perch and salmon fry. The fish immediately gathered around the lure. Although this action proved that the lure would attract, was it the vibration? Next they rigged a sheet of black plastic with fish on both sides. When they dropped the Buzz-Bomb on one side of the plastic curtain, the fish on the blind side gathered at the point nearest the lure. Obviously, the vibrations were working since the fish couldn't see the Buzz-Bomb.

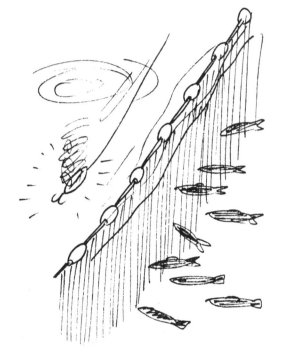

Fishing with the Buzz-Bomb is extremely simple, according to its makers. The most difficult thing is to convince anglers to follow the basic instructions. Many women, children, and fishing novices will outfish "expert" fishermen with Buzz-Bombs simply because they read and follow the instructions with each lure. These instructions tell how to "work" the lure when casting at surface-feeding fish of all types. They also describe in detail how to "mooch" or "jig" below the boat with the lure. River fishing instructions are also included.

The biggest mistake most people make is jerking the lure instead of pulling it. Salmon are not that expert at catching a lure and it should be pulled only about 18 inches or so before letting it fall free. If you give a huge jerk, the lure disappears from the salmon's range of vision.

Rex also claimed that wounded herring will sometimes dart right past a salmon. If your lure disappears in a fast jerk, the salmon might think it has gone behind him and will turn and swim in the opposite direction.

One of the reasons people jerk so hard is their belief that the Buzz-Bomb is a snagging lure. Not so, even if some fish are foul hooked. These fish, especially chums, are not expert at catching a lure (they are primarily plankton feeders) and are foul hooked as they thrash clumsily around the Buzz-Bomb.

"BUZZ-BOMBING"

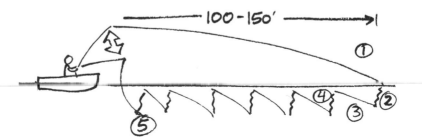

1. CAST.
2. LET BUZZ BOMB SINK A FEW FEET.
3. RETRIEVE SMOOTHLY BY RAISING ROD TIP.... **DO NOT JERK!**
4. DROP ROD TIP QUICKLY·· TO GIVE FULL SLACK LINE; REEL-IN LINE SMOOTHLY AS BUZZ BOMB SINKS.
5. CONTINUE UNTIL FULLY RETRIEVED.

The rotating, falling action between pulls is what gets them. To assure a free fall, it is important to snap the rod tip down after each pull and keep the line slack during the downward "buzz." Lift up easy on the rod at the end of the drop, and if you feel the slightest tick — hit hard.

Most success in Buzz-Bomb mooching is very close to the bottom along shelving banks. Another successful depth is 25 feet from the surface. Don't waste too much time on the in-between depths unless you see schools of feed on a sounder. Then fish just below the feed.

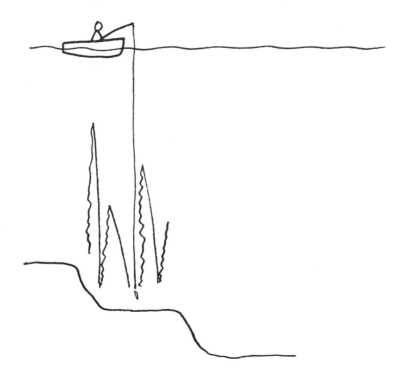

Doug Field has observed an interesting phenomenon on his depthsounder. When a large school of bait fish splits into two or more vertical sections, he says that predator fish are charging into the bait swarm, opening a hole, or "window," where the bait fish have scattered.

When this happens, Doug recommends dropping his Zzinger (or other jig) down rapidly through the blank spot in the school. Keeping a very slight tension on the line helps hold the lure vertical and allows it to descend more rapidly.

Often the fish will grab the lure as it spirals down through the bait window. Strike hard if the line stops peeling out, or even slows down a bit.

Speaking of dropping jigs rapidly, a surprising jigging technique is being used in Saanich Inlet near Victoria and other relatively sheltered areas free of fast tidal currents. The jigs are dropped straight to the bottom, sometimes 200 feet or more, then cranked to the surface as fast as the angler can wind the reel handle.

This technique sometimes works when conventional jigging techniques are fishless. I have not tried it, but it seems to have several advantages — it exposes the lure to fish at all water depths from the bottom to the surface; the fast action, in a straight vertical line, is easier for the fish to catch than an erratic jigging motion; and, finally, a lure streaking upward near a school of feeding salmon could easily trigger a fish to strike.

The faster the better seems to be the criterion for this type of jigging. One enthusiast told me he even had the gear ratio in his spinning reel increased so he could retrieve faster.

Jigging lures can also be used effectively in river estuaries and in the rivers themselves. (See page 141, "Fishing in Rivers and Estuaries.")

Conclusions from Underwater Research on Jigs

Although we found it very difficult indeed to keep jigging lures in front of our underwater camera, we have spent hundreds of hours watching salmon and other species reacting to our lures.

When we got the lures working in front of the lens, the fish came very quickly or not at all. They would look cautiously or aggressively at the lure, sometimes with several fish swarming around it.

If they were going to strike, they did it in the first two or three minutes. If not, they would lose interest and move away. We could continue to jig with the same lure in the same spot for up to an hour and they would not return.

However, if we changed lures (size, shape, or color) they returned immediately to inspect it, sometimes striking, sometimes not. If they did strike, we could usually land the fish, return to the same place with the same lure, and catch more fish.

This observation leads to an important rule for jigging. Don't keep jigging in the same place with the same lure for more than five or ten minutes if you aren't getting strikes. Either there are no fish present, or they have inspected and turned down your offering.

Change something to get results. Change your depth first, unless you are fishing needlefish schools on the bottom. Then change color, then perhaps size or shape. If nothing works, move to another location.

I've watched many expert jig fishermen who, even without an underwater camera, have reached the same conclusion. They use short jigs, sometimes one person working two rods, one with each hand. In a few minutes, they change lures. If not successful, they fire up their outboard and are gone to another location, often less than 15 minutes after their arrival.

So far as colors are concerned, we have not been able to determine any firm rules. While fish often have color preferences, we couldn't find any way to predict them. My own general rule is to use green, blue, or silver in relatively clear water, and all-white in murky water or when fishing over 100 feet deep. Shades of pink are sometimes effective when fishing shallow, especially in spring or fall when euphausid shrimps color the water. Top Buzz-Bombers claim that green or white work well on actively feeding fish. Later in the fall, charcoal and half charcoal, half grey become very effective, especially in river-mouth areas.

We were extremely pleased with the results of our underwater camera experiments which we feel shed important new information on jigging technique. Addition of a spinner tail on our own jig design produced dramatic increases in strikes, and percentage of strikes converted to "fish on."

We have been showing this startling new underwater jigging footage to our seminar audiences all over British Columbia, Washington, and Oregon. Many experienced jig fishermen are amazed at how the fish react to our lures, especially as they focus in and strike at the spinner which slows the lure's descent. (We plan to hold future seminars across Canada and the U.S. We would be pleased to send you a seminar schedule.)

Other Heavy Casting Lures
While the Buzz-Bomb was the first popular casting-jigging lure, there are now many other makes, several of them also B.C. inventions.

Doug Field has developed the "Zzinger" which rotates on the line like a Buzz-Bomb, but is fish shaped and has a unique horizontal, then vertical, flutter. Doug claims it is extremely effective for all game fish.

The Deadly Dick, developed on Salt Spring Island in the early 1950s by "Tats" Gatley, was the first of the true heavyweight lures as opposed to casting spoons. It is a diversified lure which can be cast, trolled, jigged or even mooched. It is manufactured in Victoria.

Another B.C. lure is the Rip Tide Striker, developed in the 1960s by the late Hugh Reid. He wanted a driftfishing lure which would get down through the swirling tide rips to where he knew big salmon were feeding on schools of bait. The turbulent waters of Sansum Narrows between Vancouver Island and Salt Spring Island was where he perfected the lure. It took fish over reefs and ledges where the strong tidal current prevented trollers or moochers from reaching.

We have done some interesting experiments, watching jigging lures with our underwater research camera. We found that Rex Field's advice to use short pulls instead of hard jerks was absolutely correct. Not only are short pulls more effective, but we were surprised to find that the salmon had a difficult time catching even a short pulled lure.

We attempted to design a jig which would move more slowly, adding fins to slow the descent, but the action wasn't right. We tried jigs of a lighter metal, or combination metal and plastic, but they were often swept away in the current. We finally added a forked spinner, similar to the one used on our trolling lure. It slowed the lure descent just enough for the fish to catch it more easily.

As a bonus, the spinner put out fish attracting vibrations like the Buzz-Bomb. Our camera showed the forked shape acted as a visual trigger and focused the strike right at the hook, unlike other jigs which fish often grabbed at the wrong end. Anglers using this new lure report a high percentage of strikes are solidly hooked in the jaw, as opposed to missed strikes and foul hook-ups on lures without a tail spinner.

The needlefish shaped jigs are very productive over sandy bottom areas where they imitate sand lance (candlefish, needlefish, among other names) which hover in schools right on the bottom. Bouncing any of these needlefish jigs right on the bottom can be effective in late spring and early summer.

Many jigs — Stingsildas, Pirkens, and my own The Lure-Jigging Model — are often more effective when bent into a slight "C" or "S" curve. The "C" bend improves flutter-down action and the "S" bend is good for casting from a boat, wharf, rock outcrop, or from the beach.

(Since the first edition of *Advanced Techniques*, the jigfishing-driftfishing method of fishing has grown in popularity, with many new lures and ways to use them developed. All are described in Heritage House book, *Driftfishing: The British Columbia Way*, now in its fourth revised edition.)

CHAPTER SIX By Lee Straight

Mooching (Still-fishing or very slow Trolling)

As Charles White says in his basic text, *How to Catch Salmon — Basic Fundamentals*, there are no hard or fast rules about the sport. But one of the delights is working up rules for yourself. The longer you fish,

the more rules there are and the more "hard and fast" they appear to you. I have several such firm rules, and it distresses me to see other anglers ignore them, even as they no doubt frown when I seem to ignore one or more of theirs.

Would you believe that my first rule is to close trim all knots?

My friends say that this rule stems from my meticulous nature. I say that it prevents tangles and reduces the chance of seaweed catching on my tackle. Mooching tackle in general is light. Once you're accidentally hooked into a bundle of seaweed, it is much easier to tear hook, line and sinker through it if there are no tags on the knots.

When I mooch deep, I use shorter, thicker leaders. Winter fish, being smaller, allow lighter, eight to 10-pound test leaders. Rambunctious summer cohos require no less than 10 pound, while mature summer chinooks call for no less than 15 pound. No heavier is required if you use light weights and limber rods, as they'll give with the action of the fish. But a fish soon pops thin leaders on stiff rods or heavy sinkers.

Mooching in tidal rapids with short, stiff, trolling rods has led to the use of 30- and even 40-pound test leaders because of the combination of resistant tackle, heavy current and bulky fish.

Short leaders, never more than five feet, prevent your bait, particularly if a live bait, from twisting round and round the main line

as the sinker plummets down when you're casting or just lowering your bait. When you can, pay it out carefully, moving the boat away as you do. If you always cast if far to the side, then use a leader only a foot shorter than the rod — never longer than the rod as it makes netting the fish difficult.

Mooching Sinkers, Line and Reels
Best sinkers for mooching are the crescent type. You may wish to cast some line and the crescent doesn't tangle in midair. In summer,

the best line for stripcasting is stiff or hard nylon monofilament. Stiff line lies more loosely in coils on the boat deck once the kinks are taken out of it.

Medium-stiff lines are better for winter stripcasting-mooching as the lower temperatures make hard nylon tend to kink. My favorites for winter mooching are two medium-limp lines called Stren and

Triple Fish. Both have knot strength greater than any other brand I've tested by pulling until it breaks.

Durable, hard monofilament tends to be stretchy, and have more "memory," which means you must stretch it, coil by coil, to remove the curl after it has been stored on the reel overnight or longer.

Stretchy line, however, has one redeeming feature: its extra spring takes up sudden shocks when fish change direction, thereby reducing breaks in line or leader. This feature is a noticeable advantage when the fish is some distance from the angler.

Both brands are quality lines at "quality" (high) prices. Certainly their excellent knot-strength indicates quality. They flatten out and weaken less readily in knot-tying and are less susceptible to crushing underfoot while stripcasting or mooching. They are also more resistant to nicking from flying hooks brushing them, or from scrubbing on rocks, fish scales or fish teeth.

For leader material I favor the hardest, most neutral-tinted monofilaments — hardness, to resist nicking; paleness, to fool the fish. A salmon gets a long, steady look at a leader, mooched quietly

far below, so you need all the camouflage you can get, unlike the fast-moving lure and leader.

The type of reel seems unimportant for mooching. If you like to stripcast, then a single-action reel is preferable as the handles are less likely to catch loose loops of line when stripping it into the boat. Also, single-action reels are, like fly reels, far more sporty for playing fish.

Some experts, desiring only to hide their good luck from chance nearby boats, switch off the ratchet drags on their single-action reels, leaving just slight center-pin drag to keep the reel from running wild. They wish to hide the number of pulls of line they make as they lower their bait, even faking their hand movements. And they like to play fish in silence, even to holding their rod tips in the water as long as possible. By contrast, I like to let my reel howl as a strike, far below, proves a salmon and it runs and runs.

SINGLE HOOK RIG FOR MOOCHING WITH LIVE HERRING

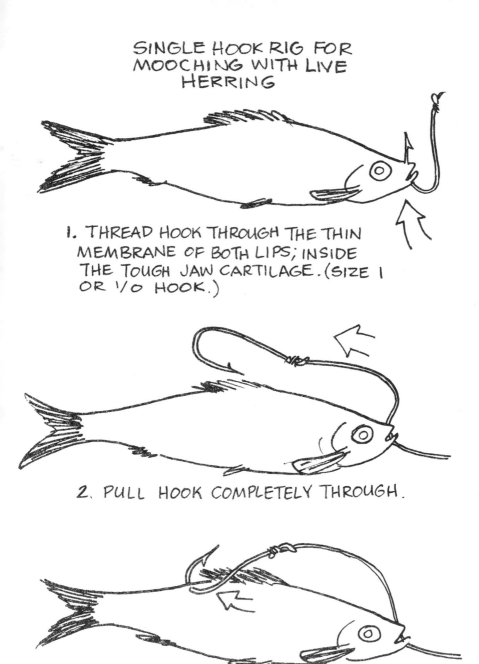

1. THREAD HOOK THROUGH THE THIN MEMBRANE OF BOTH LIPS; INSIDE THE TOUGH JAW CARTILAGE. (SIZE 1 OR 1/0 HOOK.)

2. PULL HOOK COMPLETELY THROUGH.

3. INSERT HOOK THROUGH BACK, JUST UNDER SKIN, BEHIND DORSAL FIN. BE CAREFUL NOT TO PUT HOOK TOO DEEP OR FISH WILL BE INJURED OR PARALYZED.

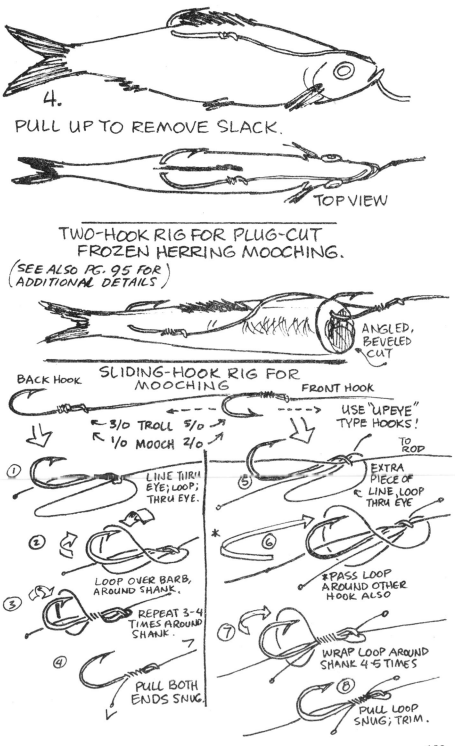

4.

PULL UP TO REMOVE SLACK.

TOP VIEW

TWO-HOOK RIG FOR PLUG-CUT FROZEN HERRING MOOCHING.

(SEE ALSO PG. 95 FOR)
(ADDITIONAL DETAILS)

ANGLED, BEVELED CUT

SLIDING-HOOK RIG FOR MOOCHING.

BACK HOOK   FRONT HOOK

USE "UPEYE" TYPE HOOKS!

← 3/0 TROLL 5/0 ↗
← 1/0 MOOCH 2/0 ↗

TO ROD

① LINE THRU EYE; LOOP; THRU EYE.

⑤ EXTRA PIECE OF LINE, LOOP THRU EYE

② LOOP OVER BARB, AROUND SHANK.

* ⑥ *PASS LOOP AROUND OTHER HOOK ALSO

③ REPEAT 3-4 TIMES AROUND SHANK.

⑦ WRAP LOOP AROUND SHANK 4-5 TIMES

④ PULL BOTH ENDS SNUG.

⑧ PULL LOOP SNUG; TRIM.

Rods and Mooching Technique

While all rods seem okay, there is a great advantage in long, limber-tipped ones for mooching. They spread the lines more and the light tips react better to live bait or to the strikes of fish. Basically, when your tip is jigging, you don't snatch up the rod and strike. You wait until it takes a deep bow or goes suddenly straight.

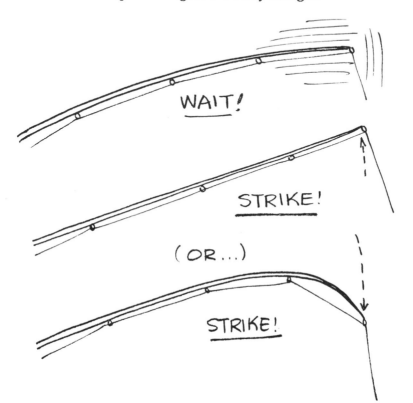

WAIT!

STRIKE!

(OR...)

STRIKE!

I use two treble hooks, tied well apart, for pure mooching. If I'm going to mix in some casting, then I like the hooks to be single. They reduce the chance of the two hooks fouling one another while sailing through the air.

I'm still undecided about actual hook size. Small, number 10 or number 8 trebles, no doubt hook more reliably but they also pull out quicker. I suspect they may be held by the fish longer since they aren't such a mouthful of metal. So I swing among sizes 6, 8, and 10, but I usually advise number 8.

Some anglers believe in pinching together two of the hooks, making a crude (and weakened) double, based on the unsubstantiated belief that the fish is less likely to throw the double hook. Suit yourself on that one. If you do remove one point of the treble, note that the third point is always soldered to a double. Cut off that third

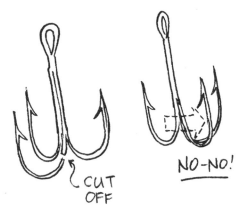

CUT OFF

NO-NO!

with pliers, rather than pinching it against one of the others.

I like herring strips large in winter, small in summer, to match the prevalent size of food. For this reason I cut them broad in winter, slender in summer, but with well shaved, sensitive tails. With live herring I always hook them in the nostrils and just back of the dorsal.

Easily the best method of mooching is with a rowboat, just "mooching" along, as the name implies. Keep your lines down at an angle of roughly 45 degrees, or halfway between vertical and horizontal, and watch your two rod-tips alternately and diligently. In

45°

ROW: Bait Rises
PAUSE: Bait Falls

power-mooching, slowing the boat is a problem. Few can hold their speed down enough to allow the lines to sink deep. Winter salmon are anywhere from 60 to 100 feet or deeper in full light, perhaps briefly at the surface at dawn or dusk. Great depth is a requirement and one of the advantages of mooching over trolling.

If you must use your more comfortable power boat in winter, then anchor. Or drift in the wind, take in your lines, motor back to

the starting point, let down the lines and drift again. In summer a few anglers catch fish by power-mooching with heavy sinkers of six to eight ounces, but seldom in winter. The lines just don't get down. If you use a planer or downrigger gurdy, that's trolling and is covered elsewhere in this book.

Here's an example of how one winter-time moocher deviates from the short leader and long rod technique. He uses a six- to 16-

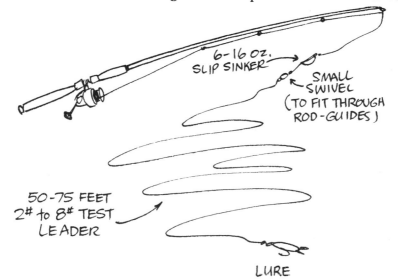

ounce slip sinker, set just above a tiny swivel, joining the mainline to a 50- to 75-foot leader of no more than eight-pound test, and as light as — brace yourself — two-pound test. He plays the fish from a short but limber trout trolling rod and free-running reel (flyreel or similar). He takes literally hours to let the fish tire, calmly and delicately removes the sinker when it comes close enough, then lets the small swivel run through the rod guides onto the reel drum. He has taken over 20-pounders in Burrard Inlet on two-pound test.

When starting, I nearly always let one line to the sea floor, then quickly wind in 20 turns to keep it clear of the bottom fish that lurk

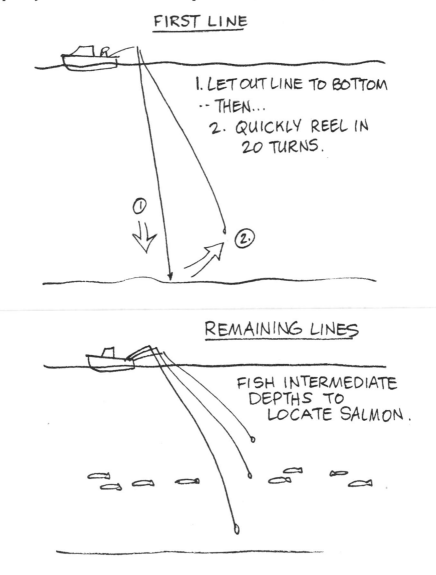

FIRST LINE

1. LET OUT LINE TO BOTTOM
·· THEN...
2. QUICKLY REEL IN
20 TURNS.

REMAINING LINES

FISH INTERMEDIATE
DEPTHS TO
LOCATE SALMON.

there. That is, unless I want a lingcod. Then I tolerate many hookups with rockfish, but try to fish where lings are found — rocky reefs in fast tides, 60 to 200 feet deep.

Lings, by the way, are no pushover and almost demand light tackle. They have prickly teeth but your thin leader usually stays in between those teeth, not cutting. A dogfish, on the other hand, rasps its way through thin leaders. "Fish light for lings" is a rule of the sport. But just take your time.

The second and other lines I lower at intermediate distances below the boat, unless anglers already on the grounds tip me off to the likely depth. This experimenting with depths is a must and one of the reasons moochers catch more salmon than trollers, once they know the area the salmon are using.

Now that we're fishing, we have long, delightfully quiet hours to idle away, one of the pleasures of mooching versus trolling. Alertness, however, is the key to success, so it isn't so sedentary a sport as it appears. Sure, snooze off if you're anchored and tired, but when you do you're settling for maybe one third the catch. Watching the rod tip tells you whether or not the fish has finally tried to swallow the bait and allows you to strike.

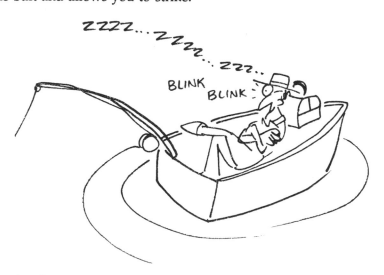

A salmon munches at a still bait, whether a strip bait or live herring, then grabs it and moves off, trying to swallow it. Your leader may block its attempt or it may detect the hard hooks and in both cases spit out the bait. It is during this interval that the alert moocher has snatched up his rod and struck, impaling the fish. That's why it is particularly important to reel speedily when the rod tip straightens, showing that even the weight of the sinker has been lifted. The salmon is heading toward the surface and you must work fast to strike it.

What's on the Line?

In waters where coarse fish abound, it is difficult to tell immediately whether or not a fish is a salmon. But salmon, once well hooked, almost invariably move off fast, slanting the line outward at a speed never matched by rockfish or dogfish, and only occasionally by lingcod. A bait struck, then dropped, showing scratches or slashes, has almost certainly been struck by a salmon. Lingcod, hake and rockfish also will slash a bait but usually just gulp it. If it's just scraped or is chopped clean, it likely was struck by a dogfish.

Once well into a fish and free of your anchor, don't be tempted to motor straight above the fish. They have more power that way, something I learned from playing halibut and later proved to my satisfaction on heavy salmon. It is better to stay to one side, dragging them off course, so to speak. They tire much more quickly. (If a fish soon sounds, then becomes immobile, it almost certainly is a lingcod

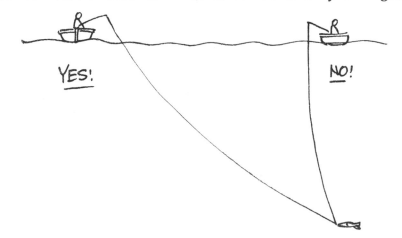

YES! NO!

or, rarely in these waters, a halibut.) You then must keep pressure on it at a wide angle, circling. It likely has its nose under a rock.

Finally, a word of advice about guiding others, usually friends from afar who've never fished at all. Or, worse, who have fished for small stuff that they're used to cranking right in.

Always, right at the start, lecture them politely and briefly about what to do when a fish strikes, letting the fish run all it likes. The worst fault of beginners is freezing on reels, then popping those light leaders we must use for mooching. Tell them you've a mile of line on the reel, that even a whale couldn't take it all in one run, then just say it's not a tug-'o-war but a trading game.

Point out that the fish takes all the line it likes while you (the beginner) just keep your rod pointed to the sky and wind line back in gently as the fish lets you. Rod high, no grabbing the reel to stop it whirling — but gentle control on the edge of it.

"Tight lines," tell them, "means a running fish, not a fish having his head torn loose."

Note from an Old Fisherman:
Never play a fish close to you. It is the surest way to lose a potential dinner. Give it plenty of room. However, the old adage is true: "If a fish wants to play, let it play in the boat."

While a salmon is dictating the battle, give it plenty of space. Once you have it under control, however, the quicker you can get it into the boat, the better.

Downrigger Fishing

This new version of an old concept has revolutionized fishing methods and dramatically increased catches for the sports troller. Except for a few months in the summer and fall when the cohos are running — and, in recent years, they seem to be running away! — trollers must go very deep to catch fish. With few exceptions, they must go deep 12 months a year to catch big chinooks.

Getting down deep used to require wire lines and heavy weights with short stiff rods to hold the weight and drag of the heavy tackle. Playing a fish properly was difficult with the unyielding rod and heavy load on the line.

Planers, which trip when you get a strike, relieve some of the

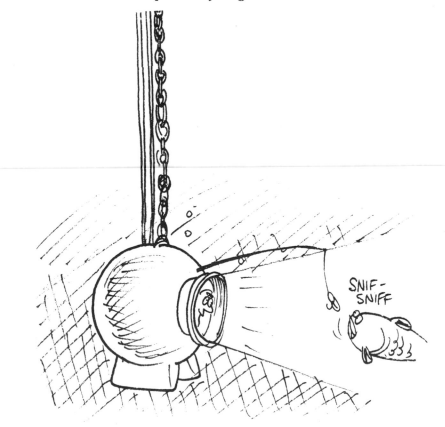

SNIF-SNIFF

pressure while playing the fish, but still require very stiff rods. Trip weights, where the lead or concrete sinker drops away at the tug of a fish, were some improvement, but still required stiff rods to hold the weight prior to the strike.

A two-rod system, with one rod to hold the weight alone, and a second to play the fish, solved a lot of the problems. They were, however, clumsy and awkward to use.

In the early 1970s, sophisticated versions of this two-rod system were developed to fish cohos in Lake Michigan. It seems the cohos, transplanted from the Pacific Coast, went very deep — sometimes more than 200 feet — seeking cooler water during the hot summer months.

These devices, called "downriggers," became very popular and

DOWNRIGGER

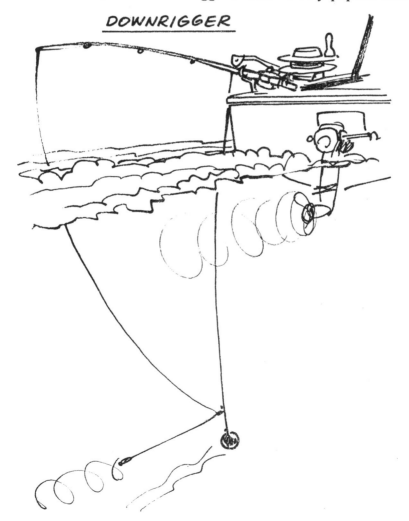

several million are now in use in North America. Essentially a compact hand gurdy, a downrigger attaches to the gunwale of the boat and carries 200 to 300 feet of wire line on its large reel. Seven to 10 pounds of lead are snapped onto the end of the wire and a release device is placed three or four feet up the wire line.

The fishing line, on a light rod and reel, is clipped to this release device and the downrigger lowered to the desired depth. When a fish strikes, the line releases and you have a fighting salmon, hooked perhaps 100 feet down, but with no weight at all between you and the fish.

Mounting the Downrigger
The downrigger plate should be mounted on the side or stern of the boat. The exact location is dependent on the shape of the boat and your fishing method. Many boats mount two, three or even four

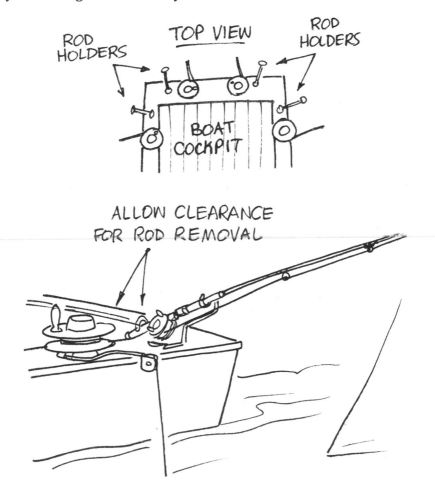

TOP VIEW

ROD HOLDERS

ROD HOLDERS

BOAT COCKPIT

ALLOW CLEARANCE FOR ROD REMOVAL

downriggers. Mounting location should allow easy access to the downrigger reel handle for winding up and down. Cranking is easiest if you can get your shoulder directly above the reel.

The rod holder should be mounted close to the downrigger, but be careful to allow enough clearance for the rod in the rod holder. Otherwise, the butt of the rod may interfere with the downrigger reel. Allow enough clearance so the rod can be easily removed from the rod holder when you get a strike.

When mounting the downrigger on the side of the boat, we find it more convenient if the rod holder is mounted astern of the downrigger. This positioning allows easy attachment of the fishing line without tangling with the wire. If room permits, mount downrigger and rod holder on a plywood or mahogany board and then mount the board on the flat top of the gunwale.

Fishing with a Downrigger
After the downrigger is mounted, snap the weight on the end of the wire line. Be very careful not to drop the weight with a slack wire. I learned to my sorrow that a free drop of only an inch or two will break the snap swivel and the weight plummets to the bottom. But

DO NOT RELEASE WEIGHT WITH ANY SLACK IN WIRE!

REEL-IN OR LOWER WEIGHT FURTHER--TO TAKE UP SLACK

not only the ball sinks. Spirits sag a bit since often a spare isn't available and weights are expensive, although some anglers cut costs by buying a mould and making their own.

With your fishing line rigged and the boat moving at trolling speed, test lure action in the water before hooking up to the release clip. It is much easier to make necessary lure adjustments. Now strip out about 15 to 20 feet of line and attach the line to the release clip.

ROD TIP

Do this prior to placing the rod in the holder or you will find it very awkward to get at the line. (I just lay my rod down with the tip near the downrigger.)

Next steps are as follows:

1: Place rod in holder then check lure action once more.

2: Confirm water depth on chart or sounder and decide how deep you want to fish.

3: Set tension on fishing reel loose enough to allow downrigger to pull fishing line down. Release clutch brake and crank out line to proper depth as indicated on depth counter. Set clutch brake when proper depth is reached.

4: Tighten fishing reel tension to overcome the drag from water friction. Your lure is now working at the exact depth you have chosen.

5: Wind in fishing line to take up slack between rod tip and release clip.

While the downrigger takes some getting used to, once the routine is mastered you'll never go back to trolling with stiff rods

GEE--IZZAT ALL THERE IS TO IT?

and heavy weights or planers. You need only one set of tackle — long limber rod with light line. I use the same outfit formerly used only for bucktailing for cohos. A good combination is an eight- to 10-foot rod with a reasonably stiff butt and very limber tip, combined with a single-action reel and 15- to 20-pound test nylon.

New 1990s technology has produced some denser nylon lines

Here's an example of how a downrigger setup looks while trolling. Note the bend in the rod, due to line drag, and the angle of the downrigger wire from the same cause. It's this angle at the downrigger which makes a free-swiveling pulley a very good idea!

which give greater strength with less diameter and line friction. I am now using a Japanese import called Siglon whose 25-pound test line is thinner than my old 20-pound line.

Using thin line relieves a lot of strain on the rod, especially when fishing at depths of 100 feet or more. It also decreases tension on the release clip, resulting in fewer premature trips.

Tips for Downrigger Fishing
Salmon are usually relatively shallow in early morning and late evening and go deeper during the day, especially chinook. In such places as Saanich Inlet on Vancouver Island, chinook are 50 to 75 feet deep in the morning and night, but drop to 90 feet or more after about nine a.m.

To find the proper depth, start where you feel the fish are most likely to be, then change every 15 minutes until you locate them. Using two or even three downriggers at once can be extremely helpful in searching. Get each at a different depth and change them regularly until you find the feeding salmon.

A depthsounder is an ideal companion to a pair of downriggers since it gives you complete control. You can fish one line 15 to 20

97-FEET...
100-FEET...
104-FEET...
126-FEET...

feet off the bottom and crank it up and down as the depth changes.

You can also fish quite effectively with a good marine chart, using land marks to fish the proper depth contours. When you are first learning downrigger fishing, it is advisable to fish in an area with a gently sloping and regular bottom. Sand or mud bottoms are also much easier on heavy weights than rocky contours. But until you establish good land marks it is a good idea to keep your weights at least 30 feet above the depth shown on the chart.

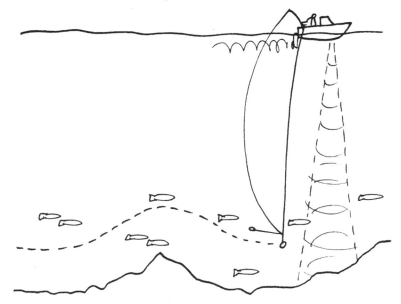

The lure should be placed at least 15 feet back from the release clip and even further back when fishing shallow. If I am fishing less than 30 feet down, I will put the lure 30 to 40 feet behind the release clip. Otherwise, the straight down pull of the weight will put the lure too close to the hull and propeller.

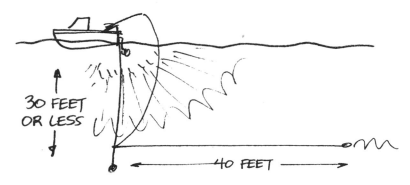

30 FEET OR LESS

40 FEET

I have always recognized that flashers and dodgers can be extremely effective at times in attracting fish and in giving that special extra "kick" to the lure. However, I hate using them because of the heavy drag they put on the fighting fish.

Hooking a flasher on a heavy leader tied directly to the downrigger ball has proved to be a very successful way of getting the advantages of a flasher without its drawbacks. The flasher is tied to a five-foot length of 80-pound-test nylon to give ample strength in the event of a bottom hang-up and also to provide stiffness, and attached directly to the swivel above the weight. Use a bead chain snap swivel for this connection to minimize twisting of the nylon.

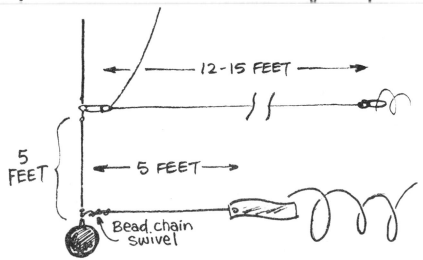

12-15 FEET

5 FEET

5 FEET

Bead chain swivel

Surprisingly, the flasher does not swing up and foul the release clip or fishing line above. They both remain parallel, even when raising or lowering the gear, provided it is down smoothly. Sudden starts and stops can cause tangles. I have been experimenting recent-

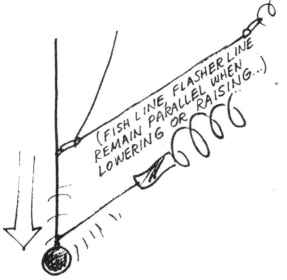

ly with longer leaders on the flasher line, usually 10 feet from weight to flasher. This set-up works well in areas where the salmon seem to prefer flashers ahead of the lure. In Juan de Fuca Strait and Barkley Sound on the west coast of Vancouver Island, chinooks are often very partial to lures towed behind flashers, and it is often difficult to catch them using a flasher on a separate line.

I'm not sure why salmon prefer flashers in front at the lure. Since these are open ocean areas, perhaps the salmon take their feeding cues from seeing other fish slashing after bait, as simulated by a flasher. The longer leader on the flasher puts the gear farther from the boat, and seems to attract more of the flasher-seeking chinooks.

The lure, on its separate line about five feet above the ball, is rigged so it trails 10 to 15 feet behind and above the flasher. For a five-foot leader, it would be 15 feet behind the wire, and up to 25 feet behind the wire when the flasher is on a 10-foot leader.

Getting a Strike
A downrigger strike differs from a conventional trolling strike since you always see the strike on the downrigger rather than on the fishing line. The jerk of the fish is transmitted up the wire line and the pulley will jerk and wiggle as the fish pulls against the release pin. The line will then (usually) pull free from the clip, your fishing line will go slack momentarily — then zing, you have a fish on the line with no weight at all.

Since there is no weight to hold the salmon down, it quite often rushes to the surface and puts up a spectacular fight right on top.

If the pin is too tight in the trolling clip, or if the fish is very small, the line may not pull free. You will usually see the downrigger wire jerking and pulling as the fish struggles against the tight clip. Grab your rod and quickly reel in until the line is very tight, then pull back sharply to free the release pin. You will be surprised at the amount of slack in what you thought was a tight line between rod and release clip. Friction drag from water passing over even thin nylon line will put quite an arc in the line which must be removed before you can get a direct pull to release the pin.

After a strike, note the reading on the depthsounder so you can get your line back to this fishy depth. Your fishing partner should reel in the downrigger while you play the fish. This reeling eliminates the possibility of the fish tangling in the downrigger line or of the weight hitting bottom if you drift into shallow water.

If fishing alone, you should get your fish under control and then wind up the downrigger with one hand while holding the rod in the other. It may be done in several segments, pausing to play the fish as necessary. In order to get the downrigger wire and weight right up to the gunwale, you will need to take off the release clip and wind the locator sleeves onto the gurdy wheel. If you are using a flasher on your weight, you will need to pull it inside the boat. As can be appreciated, landing a fish while alone leaves no time for admiring the scenery — or the fish!

You can, however, leave the weight down if no shallow water is nearby and you are careful to guide the fish away from the wire line.

Reel-in Procedure

When checking the lure after a strike, or to see why you are not getting strikes, you should trip the release clip from the boat. Most release devices will break free if you wind the line very tight then give a sharp jerk on the rod. As already noted, there is normally a little bow in the line between rod and release, so it will not trip unless this extra line is first wound in.

After the line releases, the natural tendency is to keep reeling in the line to check the lure while the downrigger weight stays down deep. One day I realized that it makes far more sense to bring up the downrigger first.

If you reel in the line, the downrigger weight is still down there and vulnerable to hitting bottom, or gathering debris. If you leave the lure in the water and retrieve the weight first, you have eliminated this hazard.

This procedure has netted me two fine fish this past season and is now a regular practice. As a friend remarked: "It's better to leave the lure in the water than that heavy weight. Not many salmon are fond of seven-pound lead balls."

More important is the fact that the lure may still be working if you leave it after tripping the release device. When the line is free, I

put the rod back in the holder and attend to the downrigger. This method allows the lure to work its way gradually to the surface and perhaps past the nose of a feeding salmon.

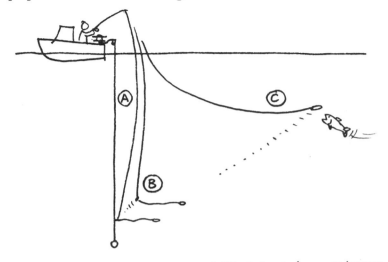

WHEN CRANKING IN DOWNRIGGER (TO CHECK CONDITION OF BAIT, ETC.): Ⓐ REEL IN FISHING LINE TO TAKE UP SLACK BETWEEN ROD AND RELEASE CLIP. Ⓑ JERK ROD TO POP LINE FREE OF CLIP. Ⓒ ALLOW LURE TO WORK ITS WAY TO THE SURFACE WHILE YOU CRANK IN THE DOWNRIGGER.
YOU HAVE A GOOD CHANCE OF GETTING A STRIKE ON THE GRADUALLY RISING LURE!

Two Lines on One Downrigger (See next page.)
It is possible to hook more than one fishing line on each downrigger. It requires separate release clips for each line and they should be attached at different depths.

Four Lines on Two Downriggers (See page 125.)
You can fish four lines from two downriggers very nicely. By spacing lures at 15-foot intervals, you can cover all depths from 40 to 85 feet at once. If you put the lures at 25-foot intervals and crank the downriggers up and down 10 to 15 feet, you can sweep all the depths over a 120-foot range.

The release clip, however, must be removable from the downrigger wire to allow winding in past the upper release. Some downrigger clips will not come off the wire easily and cannot be wound on the gurdy wheel.

If you wish to use two lines on such a downrigger, I suggest purchasing extra release clips like the Scotty or Off-Shore brands which can be placed anywhere on the wire. The clip can be snapped

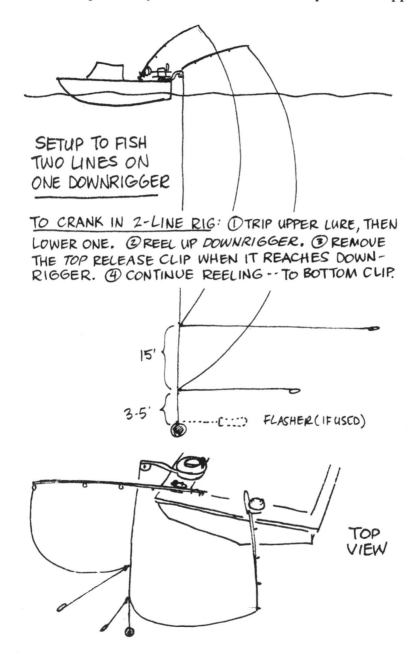

SETUP TO FISH
TWO LINES ON
ONE DOWNRIGGER

TO CRANK IN 2-LINE RIG: ①TRIP UPPER LURE, THEN LOWER ONE. ②REEL UP DOWNRIGGER. ③REMOVE THE TOP RELEASE CLIP WHEN IT REACHES DOWN-RIGGER. ④CONTINUE REELING -- TO BOTTOM CLIP.

15'

3-5'

FLASHER (IF USED)

TOP VIEW

quickly off the wire when it reaches the pulley and the locater sleeves — the soft metal sleeves squeezed on the wire to position your clip — will wind right onto the downrigger reel. These clips can be used on any make of downrigger.

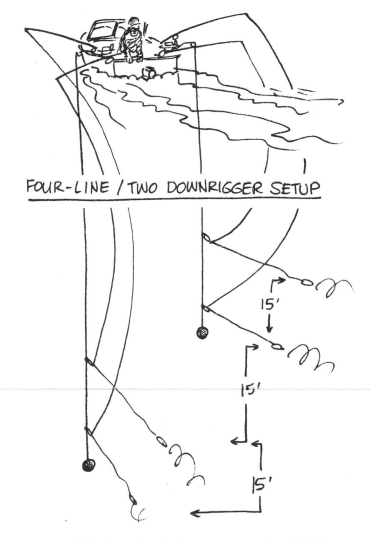

FOUR-LINE / TWO DOWNRIGGER SETUP

COVERS *FOUR* DIFFERENT DEPTHS --
eg: 15 FEET APART COVERS DEPTHS FROM
40 TO 85 FEET.

New Release Devices

The problem of detecting strikes on small fish is getting more difficult with stiffer boom arms on newer model downriggers. (See "New Developments" on page 133.) These stiffer booms don't budge on even a big strike, so I have changed the style of release clips to allow me to see these strikes on the rod tip.

These clips have a length of line between the section which attaches to the downrigger wire and the part which holds the line release. This distance makes it easier to handle the clip while it is still attached to the wire. More important, the line has more freedom of movement when a small fish strikes. This extra movement causes the rod tip to move actively and the angler can see the strike very clearly.

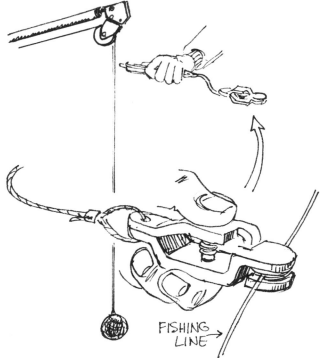

FISHING LINE →

There are several such clips on the market. Big-Jon markets the "Jettison Tripper" and Off-Shore Tackle makes a device with a leader and an alligator-type clip to hold the line. It is easy to use, trips well, and can be attached any distance from the lure.

Hitting Bottom

Bumping bottom with bulky downrigger gear can be a traumatic experience, especially if you are not used to fishing with heavy tackle. The pulley and line will sometimes start to jerk and bob in a manner similar to a fish strike.

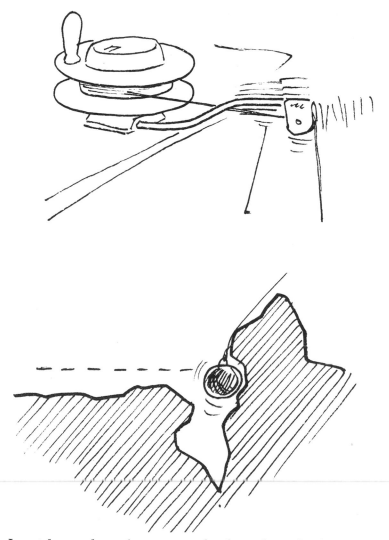

I watch my downrigger very closely and, at the first sign of a bottom hang-up, I jerk the handle back and forth sharply to dislodge the stuck weight. This action will free the weight in most cases.

If the weight is still firmly hooked on the bottom, I will sometimes back up and try to free it if the water is calm, with little tide or wind, and there is enough room to maneuver among other boats. Otherwise, I will keep jerking the handle back and forth — hard — until it breaks free, or the clip holding the weight opens up. (The weight clip on the Scotty is designed to open at a 75-pound pull.)

In this situation, you lose only the weight. If you back up, you often lose lure, flasher, swivels, and release clip. You also lose a lot of valuable fishing time while you install new clips, locater sleeves, flasher, and other gear. I keep an extra downrigger on board for just such situations. It is completely rigged, ready to go, and is snapped into place so I can continue fishing while repairing the broken unit.

Letting the line run free on a hang-up is also dangerous. The whirling downrigger handle can break your hand or arm if you grab at it in an attempt to control it.

If you break off a weight, retrieve the gear carefully as the unweighted wire line tends to ravel and may kink.

The Scotty downrigger and many other good quality brands have a slip clutch which gives more flexibility in handling bottom hang-ups. You can let the line pull out a bit and try to free it again from a different angle before resorting to breaking off the weight.

Downrigger Weights
Most downriggers come equipped with fancy, finned weights which are advertised to prevent twisting and tangling. When I started

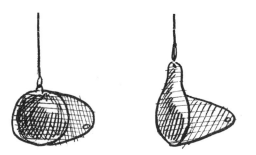

downrigger fishing, I couldn't get these weights. So I used conventional spherical leads. They worked very well.

Later on, I tested the finned weights against the much cheaper ball leads. As far as I can determine, the finned weights offer no significant advantages. If the lead is mounted below a swivel, it can't transmit any turning action to the wire. If the boat is dead in the

BEST WEIGHT UNDER NORMAL CONDITIONS IS SEVEN POUNDS --TEN POUNDS MAXIMUM!

water, both ball and fin weights will turn. When moving, neither does.

In my opinion, the round ball with the least exposed surface per ounce of weight offers less water resistance and should give greater depth. (If finned weights offered any advantage, you can be sure commercial trollers would use them. They don't.)

Finned weights sometimes have a hole in the fin for attaching a release device. I would much rather put my release device up the wire about three or four feet. If I hit bottom, only the weight is lost rather than possibly losing all the terminal tackle.

A finned weight might show up more clearly on a sounder, but I can see my ball weight well enough when I want to. If you have a depth counter on your downrigger, you don't really need to see it on the sounder anyway.

It is inevitable that you will lose weights on bottom hang-ups. When this happens, I can afford to lose two ball weights for the cost of one fancy streamlined job.

Wire Splicing
Downrigger wire can be spliced easily and quickly. If I break off a length of wire, I just splice a new wire on the remaining old wire.

1. PUT ALL SLEEVES ON LINE *BEFORE* CRIMPING ANY ...
2. CRIMP MIDDLE SLEEVE...

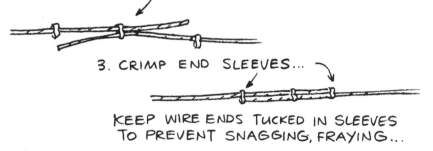

3. CRIMP END SLEEVES...

KEEP WIRE ENDS TUCKED IN SLEEVES
TO PREVENT SNAGGING, FRAYING...

Choosing a Downrigger

There are at least half a dozen downriggers on the market, ranging in price from $100 to more than $500. Some prices include wire line and others do not. Most of the models available are imported from the Great Lakes area where downrigger techiques were originally developed. Some of these units stand up well in salt-water conditions, but others will corrode and give unsatisfactory results.

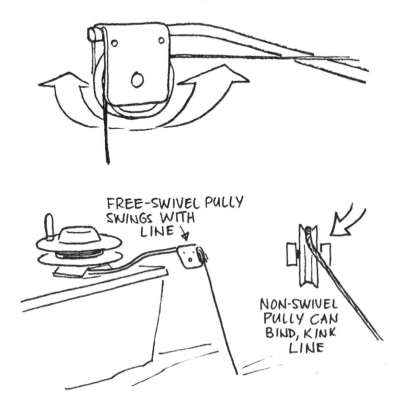

FREE-SWIVEL PULLY
SWINGS WITH
LINE

NON-SWIVEL
PULLY CAN
BIND, KINK
LINE

In choosing a downrigger, you should consider the following features:

1: Free swiveling pulley. Wire line leading from a downrigger mounted on the sides of a boat will pull back at an angle of up to 45 degrees at the water surface. (This line angle quickly becomes more vertical underwater.) If the pulley is fixed, the wire line will tend to kink at the point it takes a sharp turn under the pulley or associated guide hole.

2: Depth counter. Knowing the fishing depth at all times is one of the most important features of this type of trolling. When you get a strike, you can note the reading on the depth counter before retrieving the weight and re-set it at the same depth again. When my counter was inoperative, I tried keeping track of the number of turns on the downrigger reel and have even marked the line with small bits of yarn to measure depth. However, depths are changed regularly while fishing and it is difficult to remember the last setting in the excitement of a strike.

3: Protected depth counter. Most depth recording counters are adaptations of bicycle odometers and do not stand up well in salt water. The counter should be in an area protected from salt spray if possible. A geared counter as opposed to a pulley operated counter is also preferable.

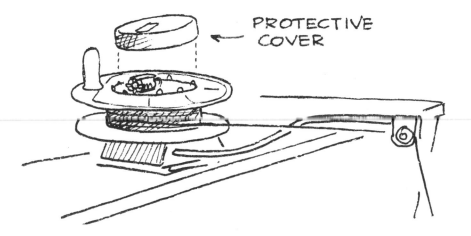

PROTECTIVE COVER

4: Mounting and dismounting. Unless you plan to leave your unit permanently affixed to your gunwale, the daily setting up can be a nuisance. Some units require bolting on to a permanent plate which takes time and risks dropping bolts overboard. Others utilize a more convenient slide-in, slide-out mounting.

5: The release device should be strong enough to hold the line in place, yet trip cleanly when the fish strikes. If possible, the line should not be pinched between metal clamps which tend to nick and

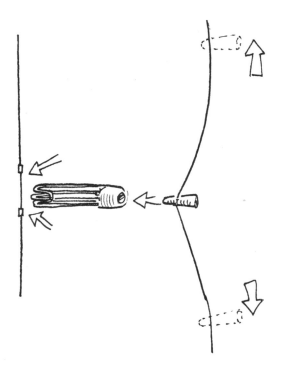

weaken the nylon line. Release pins, if used, should slide freely down the fishing line. Fixed releases force you to put the lure at a set distance from the downrigger wire. If the release device is fixed and too large to go through the rod guides, you are very limited in the distance between lure and weight. This system is often undesirable.

  6: A clutch-brake is a convenient extra which allows a smooth and easy lowering of the weight.

7: Swivel mount: Some of the more expensive units allow the entire gurdy arm to swing inboard for easy rigging and to keep it out of the way when travelling or coming into a dock.

8: Wheel mount: Most downriggers have vertically mounted gurdy wheels, but some utilize horizontal mounts. While the selection is a matter of individual choice, you should remember that vertical mounts often require separate right and left hand models for each side of the boat.

NEW DEVELOPMENTS

Downrigger technology continues to evolve and I'm changing some of my techniques accordingly:

1: Release clip. Newer clips have a length of line between the downrigger wire and the actual release. This distance makes it easier to attach the line to the release clip while still attached to the downrigger. More important, the line has more freedom of movement when a small fish strikes. This extra movement makes it much easier to see the strike of a small fish on the rod tip.

I like the Off-Shore release clip which has the long connector described above and also uses an alligator clip device to hold the line in place. It is easy to use, trips well, and can be attached at any distance from the lure.

2: Longer boom arms. They put the downrigger wire farther from the side of the boat which tends to minimize tangling between two downriggers and can help keep wire line out of the prop.

Longer arms do increase the torque on the boat's gunwale when you hang-up on the bottom, creating powerful leverage which can rip something loose — including tearing off the gunwale itself. So, be careful.

3: Electric downriggers. These sophisticated devices are changing the whole concept of deep trolling. They bring in the lead ball at the flip of a switch, eliminating the hand cranking when checking your gear or when playing a fish. As a consequence, they are wonderful in the excitement of a strike. You can concentrate on enjoying the play of the fish instead of frantically working to get downrigger gear out of the way.

Some sophisticated models are attached to tiny computers which

interface with a depthsounder. You can set them to stay five or 10 feet off the bottom and they will raise and lower on commands from the sounder.

Others are programmable to change depths in a timed sequence which can cover many fishing depths automatically.

As this edition goes to press, they are still illegal in the tidal waters of British Columbia, but are legal almost everywhere else. The Federal Department of Fisheries and Oceans will, however, grant electric downrigger permits to anyone with a medical disability. There is considerable pressure to make them legal for everyone in B.C., and I strongly support this move. Check the latest annual *British Columbia Tidal Waters Sport Fishing Guide* for current regulations governing general use of electric downriggers in tidal waters.

My favorite downrigger is the Scotty, another B.C. product made in Victoria. But I must admit that I am biased because I helped develop the original Scotty. That fact notwithstanding, to me it has all the features needed for successful and enjoyable downrigger fishing.

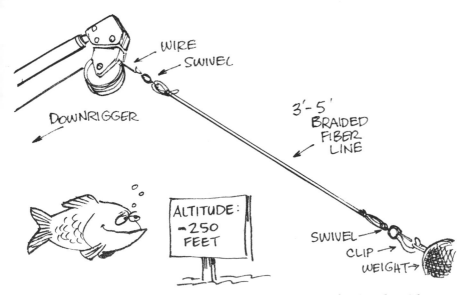

Finally, here is a tip worth trying. Some professional guides use a length of 200- to 300-pound test braided cod line between the end of the wire and the weight. Tie one end of the line to the swivel attached to the clip holding the weight and the other end to a loop in the end of the wire line. This piece of line, usually three to five feet long, makes it very easy to pull the weight in and out of the boat without cutting your hands on the wire. It also prevents kinks and frays in this most vulnerable part of the line.

CHAPTER EIGHT By Dan Stair

Planers

Gadgets which take advantage of wind, tide or wave movement have been around in the fishing world for years. At one time kites were quite popular, especially for the giant tuna off southern coastal waters in Zane Grey's day. Even before that, the Japanese used a boat-shaped wooden board with a screw eye affair in the center to pull their bone jigs through the water in their search for albacore.

Some years ago a sportsfisherman named Collins from the San Juan Islands carved up an interesting wood diving gadget that would theoretically take a lure down deep. When a fish struck the lure, it would trip and offer no resistance to the fish. Having a fishing date with his partner at Neah Bay, he decided to try it there. Upon arriving at Neah Bay, he showed his invention to Mel Ray, owner of Mel's Resort.

Mel told Collins: "If that crazy lookin' thing can catch a salmon, I'll eat it raw!"

Mel ought to know. He was a commercial fisherman for years. But, fate was against him that afternoon. The two fishermen returned to make Mel Ray eat his words. There is still a large color

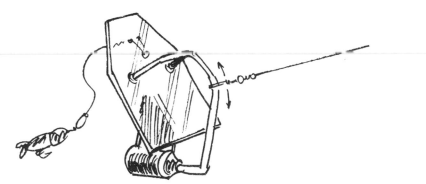

photo on the wall of Mel's Resort. It shows him eating a fresh coho salmon with some ketchup on it.

Collins did additional research on his diving planer, patented what features he could and named his invention the "Pink Lady." To date, there have been over one million of them used by sport fishermen on both Atlantic and Pacific Coasts.

Diving planers will get your gear down very efficiently, using the force of the current against the planing surface which is angled toward the bottom. Since these devices are much more than merely a means of getting a lure down to where the fish are, let's take a

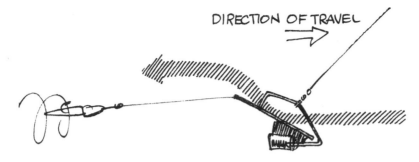

DIRECTION OF TRAVEL

WATER PRESSURE PUSHES
PLANER DOWN...

look at some of the advantages that make them so popular with salmon fishermen.

Once a fish strikes, the planer trips and offers much less resistance. Salmon are attracted to fluorescent finishes such as cerise and chartreuse, so there's a better chance of fish seeing the bait trailing

... FISH STRIKING "TRIPS" PLANER,
SHIFTS ANGLE...

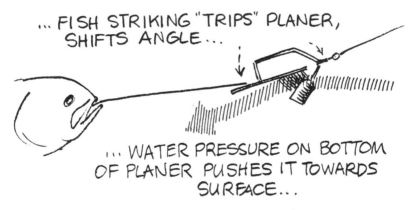

... WATER PRESSURE ON BOTTOM
OF PLANER PUSHES IT TOWARDS
SURFACE...

along behind the brightly colored planer. There's considerable merit to the theory that the turbulence of water created behind the planer excites the fish, triggering it to strike the bait. Another advantage is that the diving sinker holds the lure relatively close to the boat, allowing tight maneuvering near rocks or underwater shelves.

They also have a built-in alarm system. They are designed to trip upon bumping bottom, or when debris or seaweed foul the lure, or a fish nibbles, bringing your tackle to the surface behind the boat. This tripping at the slightest nibble is a definite advantage in chinook salmon fishing. Many lunkers will swat the lure and then

move in for the kill. When a bait fish is crippled, it often heads for the surface. When the diving sinker trips, up goes the planer and bait — a salmon, hopefully, in pursuit.

Using a planer is different from any other type of fishing. If you don't know the tricks of the trade, you won't do as well as others around you. For instance, don't use too heavy a line. It will create more water resistance and cut down depth. For salmon, a premium quality 20-pound test monofilament is ample. When attaching your main line to a diving sinker, a jam or improved cinch knot will usually do the job. Tie the main line directly to the swivel on the planer.

Addition of any extra snaps or swivels will cause the planer to

SUGGESTED DIVING SINKER HOOKUPS

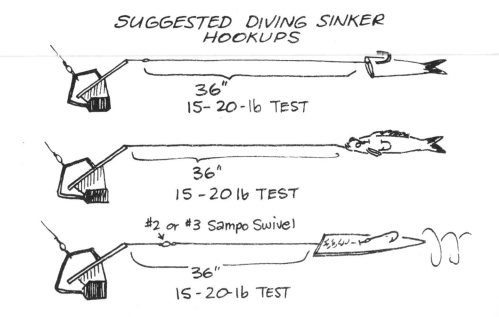

36"
15-20-lb TEST

36"
15-20 lb TEST

#2 or #3 Sampo Swivel

36"
15-20 lb TEST

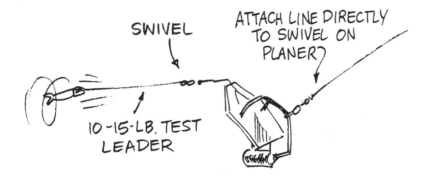

SWIVEL

ATTACH LINE DIRECTLY
TO SWIVEL ON
PLANER

10-15-LB. TEST
LEADER

change its attitude in the water and it will not function to its maximum ability. Do not attach any sinkers or attracting devices between the diving sinker and the fishing rod on the main line. These divers work well as they are and any additional weight or pull will make them trip inadvertently.

At the business end of the diver, use any rotating lure such as herring — spinner, plug-cut, or whole. Dodgers, flashers and lures or baits with actionizer heads and spinner-bucktail combinations are effective. A 10- or 15-pound test leader will allow the lure to produce maximum action. When using light leaders check frequently for line twist and abrasion. Inspect swivels for any possible fouling by seaweed or jellyfish. Change leaders after each salmon to be ready for that big one which may come along. A ball bearing swivel between planer and lure will do wonders to eliminate leader twist.

Now, let's assume you are in the boat ready to start trolling. First, adjust the throttle so the lure picks up the right fish-catching action. If more than one rod is being used, all should be checked in the water at the same time since the total force of several planers

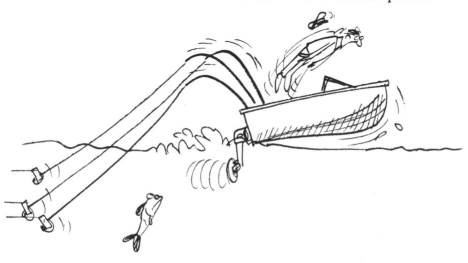

can change your boat's speed after the lines are out. It is highly recommended that the line be let out in "pulls" (one pull is about 18 inches, from reel to first guide). Slowly feed out the line to keep your gear from tangling and be alert for strikes on the way down. When not sure of the exact depth to fish, try to get one lure close to bottom and the other about 35 feet below the surface. Once the line is out, drag should be checked again before placing the rod in its holder.

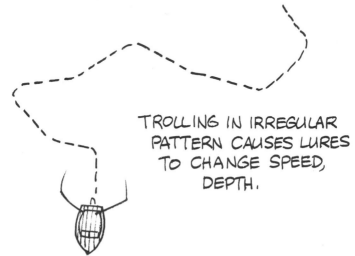

TROLLING IN IRREGULAR PATTERN CAUSES LURES TO CHANGE SPEED, DEPTH.

    Trolling in an irregular zig-zag pattern causes lures to change speed and direction, often coaxing more strikes. Shifting the trolling engine into neutral from time to time will also produce the occasional salmon. By fishing with the tidal flow, then turning around and trolling into it, productive salmon water can be much more effectively covered. Often chinook will face into the tide to feed. A good trick to turn a nibble into a solid strike is to change the length

of the leader when no action is apparent. Salmon are funny critters. The long leader or fast action bait that causes them to strike with abandon today will cause them to ignore it the next day Maybe a slow wobbler and very short leader will be the killer then. That's fishing!

When buying a diving sinker, read the instructions carefully so you will know if it will do the job you want. Some will dive deeper, pull harder, won't tow a flasher, will trip from the boat for easy retrieve, won't trip on small fish, and other variables. Known fish producers are the Pink Lady, Dolphin Diver and Deep Six.

The following chart gives an indication of depth reached by the Dolphin Diver with various line diameters and line lengths:

LINE LENGTH →	25 Ft.	50 Ft.	75 Ft.	100 Ft.	150 Ft.	200 Ft.	250 Ft.	300 Ft.
Size One 10 Test	16	31	44	57	75	83	85	–
15 Test	15	29	42	54	70	76	–	–
20 Test	14	27	39	50	64	68		
30 Test	13	25	36	46	58	60		
40 Test	12	23	33	42	52	–	–	–
Size Two 10 Test	–	NOT recommended with No. 2 Model					–	–
15 Test	17	33	48	61	83	101	116	120
20 Test	16	31	44	55	75	91	104	107
30 Test	15	29	40	49	67	81	92	94
40 Test	14	27	36	43	59	71	80	81

ACTUAL LURE DEPTHS

CHAPTER NINE By Charlie White

Fishing in Rivers and Estuaries

As salmon approach their spawning rivers, their feeding habits become erratic. Finally, they usually stop feeding altogether. Gathering in the bays and inlets where their home rivers pour into the sea, they begin milling around, sometimes in large schools and right near the surface. Cohos, especially, begin jumping and slashing all over the bay, bringing wide-eyed gasps of admiration and anticipation

from anglers nearby.

However, this time of the year is probably the most frustrating for beginner and expert alike. You have solved the problem of finding the fish. You know they are there because the damned things are

jumping all around you. But very often they just won't bite — on anything!

No one knows for sure why salmon jump, or why they jump so often near the river mouths. The most logical explanation is that they are trying to knock off pesky sea lice before they begin the upstream battle to their spawning beds.

Another, more romantic theory, is that they are jumping for joy at their successful arrival at the stream of their birth. Even more exciting, they may be eagerly anticipating their once-in-a-lifetime moment of love. Whoopee! Tonight's the night!

GEE--I'VE GOT THIS SPLITTING *HEADACHE, DEAR.....*

How, then, can we divert their attention from this powerful instinct which is apparently erasing completely their urge to feed? They do strike at lures and bait, but examination almost always reveals an empty stomach.

Did they strike out of anger at the lure coming too close, and because of annoyance at the continuing parade of lines being dragged in front of them? Many old-timers are convinced that such is the case. I believe it is true at least some of the time.

Live and frozen herring are often deadly in river-mouth areas. Could the reason be that the salmon are striking out to protect their eggs? They must develop some instinct to fight back against the predators, primarily cutthroat trout, that steal their eggs on the spawning beds. (Some trout are said to deliberately bump the ripe females to dislodge the eggs.) It is possible the salmon, especially the

big chinooks, strike at herring baits in response to this protective instinct.

The most logical theory, however, was expressed to me by Fisheries Officers at Rivers Inlet, a famous trophy fishing area in Northern B.C. where some of the world's largest chinooks gather to spawn. Several of the Officers feel that a salmon nearing a spawning river, while not feeding actively, will accept a bait presented within easy reach.

M-MM! IF THAT TASTY-LOOKING THING WAS ONLY AN INCH CLOSER...

This assumption perhaps explains the empty stomachs of mature chinooks. If a salmon will not actively chase its natural food, it is not likely to get any food. The lures and baits on our line, however, are not like a lively bait fish. We fish them very slowly, with the bait rolling over lazily. We give the chinook every opportunity to bite if it has any inclination.

We give it that opportunity over and over again as we troll or mooch our lines past its nose time and time again. With thousands of boats crowding most river-mouth areas, a fish would have to have his mouth wired shut to resist all passing temptations.

Herring Methods

While practices vary from area to area, the most successful means of catching chinooks in estuary areas is with a slow-moving bait. Herring — live, plug-cut, or whole frozen — are by far the most productive lures.

Rigging herring baits is a matter of individual preference, with many variations, even among experts. Almost all strive for the same result — a lazily rolling bait moving very slowly, or jigged slightly when mooching. Some moochers anchor and let the tide work the

bait. Others motor in reverse (the boat moves slower that way) and put the motor in and out of gear to slow the action even more. (For fishing live herring, see page 98, "Mooching.")

My own experience is almost exclusively with trolling, so the following discussion will deal with that aspect of river-mouth fishing.

Many of the pros feel it is important to bury the hooks in the herring, minimizing the metal contact when the salmon takes his

tentative munch. This "mouthing" strike, very common in fishing big chinooks, is tricky for anglers used to the savage jerk of the active feeders. It calls for patience and willpower when you realize a big one is testing your offering. When the rod bends solidly, with a soft

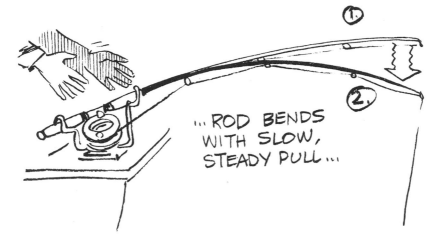

... ROD BENDS
WITH SLOW,
STEADY PULL ...

but steady pull (or, in mooching, when it goes slack), that's the moment to set the hooks with a sharp jerk on the rod.

For holding herring bait my preference for big chinooks is the plastic-headed Super Herring Teaser by Rhys Davis (called Herring

SUPER HERRING
TEASER

Aid in the U.S.). In my opinion, this "nose cover" for the herring, with its properly located front hole for the nylon line and slightly curved sides, greatly simplifies the problem of getting proper action from the bait.

It is also more likely to survive weed-fouling, or a bump on the

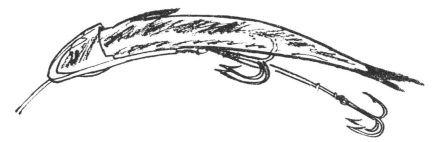

bottom. Plug-cut or unprotected whole herring are easily ruined as a bait after hitting bottom, while the Teaser keeps the herring fishable.

This method requires more hook showing. I even trail a second treble hook at the tail to get the short-biter. Evidently the fish don't mind the hooks protruding since we usually get more than our share of fish.

Sharp Hooks

I insist on keeping all hooks "sticky-sharp." Any curious salmon nosing up to the herring can easily be zapped by one of those revolving sharp points and the battle is on.

Many years ago my wife played a 40-pounder, hooked in the

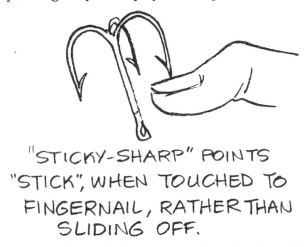

"STICKY-SHARP" POINTS
"STICK", WHEN TOUCHED TO
FINGERNAIL, RATHER THAN
SLIDING OFF.

dorsal fin, for 45 minutes before we lost it at the boat. Three times we tried to ease it those last few feet to the waiting net, but watched in horror as the hook kept tearing gradually through the thin membrane in the fin. Finally, it parted and I made a lunge for the

played-out fish as it wobbled slowly away on its side. We stared in disbelief, then looked dejectedly at each other while my wife mumbled something about lousy guides who can't even hook fish in the mouth.

On another occasion, my son hooked and landed a 42-pounder with a sharp hook imbedded under the skin of the caudal peduncle (the back end of the fish just ahead of the tail).

Proper Depth
Finding the proper depth for chinooks in river-mouth angling seems to be like all the other problems in fishing — there aren't any hard and fast rules. Each area has some most likely depths, varying from

the 10- to 15- foot range at Rivers Inlet to the 75- to 135-foot depth at Cowichan Bay.

Even these suggestions will have wide variations. But the old "common sense" and "observe what's going on" edicts will help you here. At Rivers Inlet, for example, the fish seem to lie just under a seven- to 10-foot layer of milky fresh water feeding into the bay

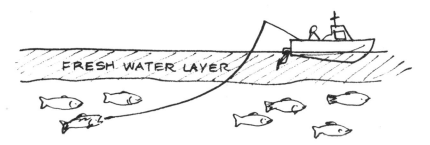

from the glacial rivers nearby. The milky layer cuts light penetration considerably, bringing the fish up.

An ideal way to locate proper depth is with a depthsounder, of course. I find my sounder most effective in this river-mouth situation. The large chinooks are gathered in schools, roaming slowly around the estuary area. They show up plainly on the sounder, so you can determine accurately both the depth and the size of the school.

It is surprising how fast this "fishy" depth can change, often with no logical explanation. I was fishing Cowichan Bay many years ago and the sounder showed a good concentration of fish at 130 feet.

Lowering my downriggers quickly, we had a solid strike almost immediately. My fishing partner played and landed a beautiful 32-pound fish, and we headed back to find the school again. We had taken some shore range markers but had drifted perhaps a half-mile in the 20 minutes of playing the large chinook on light gear.

Because the fish were not evident on the sounder when we returned, we set the downriggers at 110 and 130 feet in anticipation of finding the school at the same depth. We trolled around for about five minutes when suddenly a large concentration of blips appeared on the sounder. To my surprise, they were now at about 85 feet, almost 50 feet shallower than a half hour before.

Cranking frantically, I managed to get one downrigger up to the proper depth before we moved out of the school. We were rewarded with another strike and had our second good fish of the morning.

Without the sounder, however, we would have trolled at the wrong depth and probably drawn a blank that morning. It is just one of many examples of the unpredictable behavior of salmon. Logic would have the fish going deeper, or certainly remaining deep, as the morning wore on. This experience is one of my reasons for be-

coming more scientific and relying more on such mechanical aids as depthsounders and downriggers to achieve accurate depth control.

Time of Day
Chinooks are most likely to bite in early morning — between that first wink of daylight and the first slack tide. When I was a charter

guide, my parties used to grumble as they boarded my boat in Sidney 45 minutes before daylight. During the pitch black run over to Cowichan they would make jokes about being the only idiots in the world awake at that hour.

As we began to troll slowly in the bay, my charter guests would be startled to see other boats nearby. Then, as the light level increased, be absolutely amazed to see a panorama of 200 to 300 other boats packed into this small area. One guest remarked that it reminded him of his Navy days when they would wake up to find a

convoy of ships stretching to the horizon in all directions.

At any rate, the early morning start seems to pay off well enough to keep this pre-dawn scene repeating itself year after year. The fish are often quite shallow for the first half hour or so. When the bays are not too crowded, I have found big chinooks as shallow as 20 to 25 feet. But as mentioned, Rivers Inlet and other glacial river mouths are the exception. Here salmon are 10 to 15 feet down most of the time. However, as most areas are becoming overcrowded, the hundreds of whirling props and thumping engines seem to be driving fish deeper, even at the crack of dawn. I'm finding that 50 to 70 feet is often productive at daylight in these wall-to-wall boat situations.

Sun Up — Fish Down
Notwithstanding my story about the salmon school coming up from 130 feet to 85 feet, the normal experience is for fish to drop deeper as

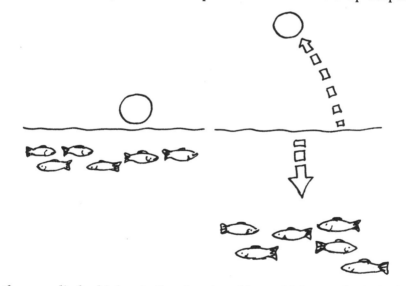

the sun climbs higher in the sky. Anything which cuts the light level — fog, cloud, rain, muddy water — tends to keep the fish shallower.

If you see another fish taken, by all means talk to the successful angler. It is an excellent way to short cut your depth experimenting. If you can, mark the location. Every bit of data will help you solve some of the many unknowns.

Evening fishing is productive in some estuary fisheries, but rather poor in others. Local knowledge in each area is the only way to find out if it's worth firing-up the motor after dinner.

Sun Down — Fish Up
The fishy depth in the evening is the reverse of morning conditions.

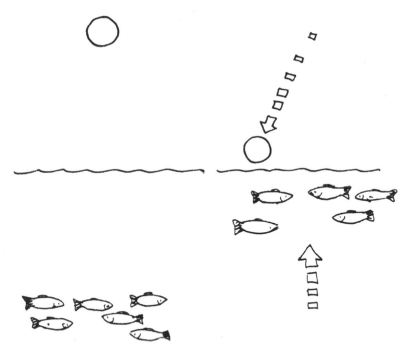

As the light level drops, salmon move toward the surface. Just as the sun is setting, the evening quiet will often be broken by some excited shouts and screaming reels.

Sometimes the most productive time of all is after most of the boats have gone in for the night. I've caught some real lunkers when we stayed out for one more pass over my favorite spot, often landing (or losing) the fish in complete darkness. Many excited anglers join the group already at the dock with wide-eyed stories of the terrific strikes they got while trolling home in gathering darkness.

Maybe the salmon comes up to the surface when all the noise and confusion dies down, and is more likely to swipe at the dimly-seen lure rolling lazily past its nose. Staying out that extra half hour

PHEW!

is sometimes difficult after a long day on the water, especially when you know you will be getting up in the dark again the next morning. But sometimes it pays off.

River-mouth Cohos

Catching spawner cohos is even more challenging than tempting the big chinooks. The cohos' greater tendency to jump and more erratic striking behavior are enough to drive even the most patient sportsman wild with frustration. Especially after he has trolled through a

large school of leaping cohos again and again with nothing but seaweed grabbing his hooks.

This all-too-common experience has led many fishermen to repeat the old wives' tale that salmon don't bite when they jump. They'll bite — sometimes — if you give them that special something that triggers their instinct to strike. In fact, jumping fish are the first thing to look for when going after cohos.

While expert river-mouth anglers have differing theories on how to make cohos strike, they usually agree on the first step — find the jumpers! The late Lee Hallberg, one of the real pros who taught me a lot about Cowichan Bay, made a regular practice of counting jumpers for a few minutes before putting out his lines.

He divided the bay into several areas or segments, and counted for a minute or so the jumpers in each location. Then he headed for the greatest concentration. Incidentally, Lee's wife, Paddy, still holds the world record for cohos with a 31-pounder she landed at

Cowichan Bay.

Bruce Colegrave, another top expert, scans the area regularly with binoculars to look for jumpers, rollers or fish finning on the surface. Since cohos are restless, fast-moving fish, these signs of their presence are almost essential for consistent success.

Speaking of signs, I've found that gull activity is not as reliable a fish indicator in river-mouth areas. The salmon are not actively feed-

ing and seldom, if ever, drive up the herring for the gulls to feed on.

After finding the coho schools, give them a variety of lures to see which tempts them. My favorite is a bucktail fly. I often put out four different colors until we find which they prefer. A good sized abalone spinner in front of the fly gives it an extra wiggle and at-

155

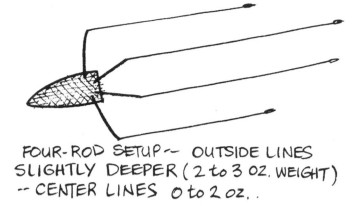

FOUR-ROD SETUP — OUTSIDE LINES
SLIGHTLY DEEPER (2 to 3 oz. WEIGHT)
-- CENTER LINES 0 to 2 oz.

tracting flash. My preference is the No. 4 Cowichan Style Abalone made by Radiant Lures in Victoria.

Zig-zagging back and forth with a sharp, 45-degree turn every 200 feet or so gives lures extra action. The outside fly speeds up as it travels around the larger outside arc, like "cracking the whip" in a row of ice skaters. The inside fly hesitates and drops down as the pull from the inside rod slackens. Both changes in action will often

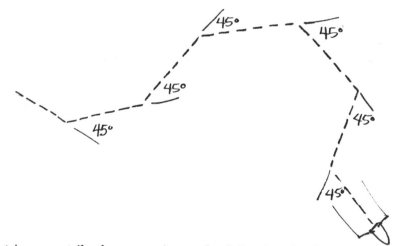

trigger a strike from a curious coho following the fly.

There are many theories on how to choose the color and size of fly for river-mouth trolling. The majority of high-liners seem to prefer a larger, bushier fly than that used on feeding cohos. Some, however, stay with the medium-sized flies and do very well. These medium flies are often those with bright aluminum colored mylar wrappings and fluttering "tails" beneath the hair. Radiant Lures make an excellent selection of this type of fly.

Colors vary tremendously. Some anglers stick with three or four

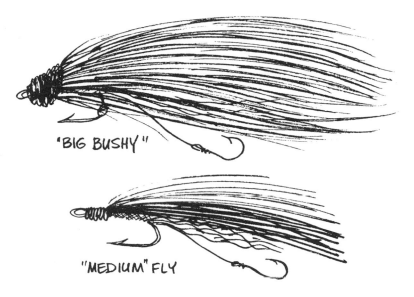

"BIG BUSHY"

"MEDIUM" FLY

basic colors, while others try every shade and combination available. Blue and white, Grey Ghost (grey and white), Coronation (red, white and blue), and sometimes pink and white seem to be the old standbys. The "big and bushy" advocates seem especially fond of those combinations.

I have switched in recent years to medium flies because I've built up a fairly complete color selection. A bluish-purple fly called Ol' Smoky has been effective late in the season after mid-October. A bright yellow or pure white is sometimes productive, especially on a dark, rainy day. Pink- or ginger-colored flies can be deadly earlier in the season when fresh runs are arriving. The cohos must remember the tasty, pink-colored shrimps they were eating recently.

One local expert is convinced that washed-out, faded colors are

the real killers. He even leaves his new flies, wet with sea water, in the sun to bleach — just like my teenagers did with their new Levis.

Faded colors often work very well for me. I have two faded old blue-and-whites (the blue is almost gone in one of them), and a washed-out pink which produce year after year. However, I wonder! Is it the faded color, or is the construction of these flies somehow different?

We all have noticed that putting out two, or even three, apparently identical flies will not produce equal results. More often than not, one fly will get all the strikes. I've had seven or eight straight strikes on the same pink fly with two other pink flies out at the same time. If I switch the productive fly from one side to the other, or straight down the middle, it still gets all the strikes.

Surely there is something a little different about this particular fly — perhaps some slight color variation. But, more likely, its action is probably slightly different in the water. Perhaps it is because of some variation in the thickness, length or placement of the hair, mylar, or thread wrapping. One top bucktailer, who ties his own flies, puts a huge, bulging head of thick thread wrapping on the front of his flies. He claims it greatly increases their productivity.

If one fly continues to out-produce others of a similar color, naturally you will use it more often. Soon it will begin to fade and

bleach from the continued exposure. Soon all your productive flies are faded, but that's not why they were effective in the first place. However, that's just one opinion. Maybe the bleached flies are more effective because of the faded color.

Trolling Speed
Trolling speed can vary when trying to outwit the fussy cohos. As a generalization, faster speeds are more successful. But, as usual, the ornery cohos just won't be typecast into any mold. I usually start out at a reasonably good clip then watch — not wait — for developments.

If I get a good strike, fine, I'm at the right speed. If not, I watch to see if anyone else is scoring. If someone catches a fish I try to

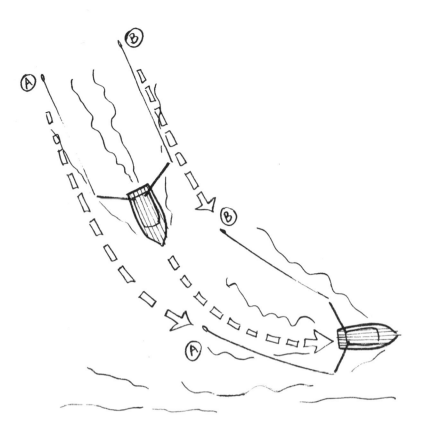

AS BOAT TURNS, LURE Ⓐ ON OUTSIDE
OF TURN, MOVES THROUGH WATER FASTER,
TENDS TO RISE CLOSER TO SURFACE.
LURE Ⓑ, ON INSIDE, GOES SLOWER, DEEPER.

learn his successful fly color, then pace myself at a reasonable distance from him. If no one is getting fish, I will continue a zig-zagg pattern and change fly colors every 10 minutes or so.

If I get a strike, or even a light touch on the outside fly on a turn, I'll speed up since this action indicates preference for a faster-moving lure. If they take the slow inside fly, I'll cut my speed. Because the fly also tends to sink on the inside turn, I may also add a bit more weight.

If fishing is particularly slow or if jumpers are scarce, speeding up to almost ridiculous speeds often is productive. An old pro at Cowichan told me he always tries to go twice as fast as the other boats. The faster speed, he believes, makes a lure stand out and cohos are more attracted to it. Problem is, if everyone adopted this philosophy, we'd soon have unlimited hydroplanes screaming around the bays and inlets.

We are not sure why such a fast speed works. But there is no question that it often does — and well. Sometimes, I will troll at six or seven miles an hour or even faster. My 24-foot, deep-vee boat will actually begin to lift its nose to start toward a planing speed. At this speed you must be very alert to avoid collisions or line-tangling with slower boats. Such speeds can also cause an annoying wash under crowded conditions.

A strike at very fast speeds is a jolting experience. The coho grabs the fly in a darting lunge and takes off in the opposite direc-

tion. The sudden high-pitched scream of the reel startles even the most blase' fisherman. In fact sometimes the rod will snap back so violently that it almost jumps out of the holder.

I have had a rod actually leap out of a holder pointed directly astern of the boat. For this reason, unless you have rod-holders that grip the rod securely, it is a good idea to tie a safety line on any rod pointed aft.

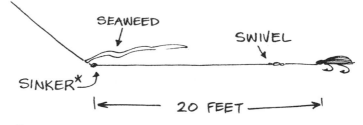

SEAWEED

SWIVEL

SINKER*

|← —— 20 FEET ——→|

* 1-3 oz. FOR AVERAGE TROLLING SPEED --
TO 5-6 oz. FOR HIGHER SPEEDS.

Normally, I put an ounce or two of lead about 20 feet in front of each fly to hold it slightly under the surface. More important, the weight tends to catch small bits of weed and other debris which would otherwise foul the spinner or fly. Three or four ounces is as heavy as you generally need when bucktailing, unless going very fast.

At these faster speeds, you might go to six ounces. Even in this situation, however, four ounces is usually enough.

Other Coho Lures

While bucktailing is the most exciting, and often the most productive, method of catching cohos at river mouths, there are several other successful techniques. These include trolling with bait, plugs, and spoons; mooching with bait or jigging or casting with Buzz-

Bombs, Deadly Dicks, Sneaks, Bolo's, Metrics, or my Charlie White jigs.

The Apex spoon is becoming more popular, as is my The Lure — Trolling Model. Both of these lures can be fished successfully with or without a flasher.

In trolling with bait, faster speeds as in bucktailing are often successful. While we don't use the already mentioned "planing speeds," often herring strip or minnow can be whirling at a dizzying pace. The problem is slowing it down so cohos can recognize it. This

slowing usually can be done by using Super Strip Teasers, pulling the hooks back to the tail of the bait, or straightening the curve of the plastic head by steaming it over a kettle.

Smaller plugs and spoons, in weird and wonderful colors, are often effective for cohos. Try to get plugs or spoons designed for fast troll, or watch your regular spoons and plugs for the fastest speed at which they still give proper action. (See page 75, "Plug and Spoon Techniques.")

Flashers and dodgers, in some instances, will increase catches on spoons and flashtails. But don't get your hopes too high. On other occasions, flashers seem to scare the fish away. If you want to use flashers, fish them the same way as with feeding cohos, except perhaps with a little longer line between flasher and lure. (See page 84, "Dodger-Flasher Trolling.")

As the season progresses past mid-October, cohos tend to change their habits somewhat. The fresh runs arriving at the estuaries are often a larger, huskier variety with their noses beginning to hook. They show a hint of pink or grey on their sides and belly, but are often the wildest fighters of the year.

When my normal tactics do not produce fish at this time of year

(if even my Ol' Smoky lets me down) I will resort to a trick taught me by the late Mr. Ordano, the dean of boathouse operators at Cowichan. One day many years ago I wasn't having any luck and asked Ordano what to do.

He pulled out a big Flatfish (U-20) that was bright orange and covered with black spots. "Try this," he said, with a wink. "No charge if it doesn't work, but you'll have to replace it if it gets chewed up."

Two hours later, I returned with three lovely cohos totalling over 35 pounds and a very scarred Flatfish. I was delighted to replace it and buy a couple more. Ever since then I have kept a big orange Flatfish with my bucktail flies for use after mid-October. The orange and black-spot combination seems to work on many lures from mid-October to late November.

An enterprising friend uses very small Flatfish trolled 40 feet deep (I put mine down only 10 to 15 feet with a four-ounce weight) with consistent late season success. He even caught several large chinooks by painting the plastic head of a Strip Teaser with orange and black spots. Maybe it reminds the fish of salmon eggs and somehow stimulates them to strike.

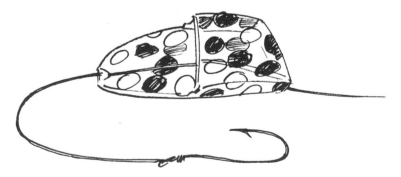

Estuary Casting

Casting weighted lures with a spinning outfit is good exercise and can provide exciting sport. If possible, cast the lure into a school of jumpers, let it drop down, then retrieve a short distance and let it drop down again. (See page 90, "Jigging-Driftfishing Lures.")

Sneaks, Metrics, Deadly Dicks, the Charlie White jig and similar

LUHR JENSEN
"SNEAK"

lures are effective in shallow areas along the edges of bays and at river mouths. In addition, any lure with a big spinner seems to produce cohos in river mouths or even in the rivers themselves.

Mooching
Mooching for cohos with herring bait in estuary areas has met with only very limited success. Mooching, being a more or less stationary fishing method, is not active enough for the fast moving cohos as it is in the tidal areas of the open Strait of Georgia.

Dark Fish
River-mouth fishing will sometimes yield salmon which have darkened considerably. These fish, usually with severely hooked noses, are not attractive looking. Many fishermen wonder whether or not they should throw them back. With the price of meat and the scarcity of fish, they are sorely tempted to keep them, but worry about flesh quality and the hoots of derision from other anglers.

Flesh condition is a relative thing. When I lived on the Snake

River near Lewiston, Idaho, local anglers used to bring home salmon that looked as if they had been run over by a freight train — and had leprosy before that. They were torn and scarred with big, open sores on their bodies. These chinooks were almost on the spawning beds after a more than 400-mile swim up from the Pacific Ocean.

I was appalled at their condition, but the local angler would

remark about the fish being in "nice shape" and tell me about its good table quality. I wondered if perhaps he meant that it tasted like the table top!

At any rate, those fish were in far worse condition than any sal-

mon still in salt water. Certainly the flesh is edible on any dark fish you catch, and is likely still of good quality. If you think one is in really bad shape, try having it smoked. I guarantee it will be delicious that way. Many Indians use these spawners as a staple part of their diet.

Chums, Sockeye and Pinks

These salmon species are also taken in river-mouth areas, but the techniques for sockeye and chums are highly specialized. Chums used to be considered uncatchable with sport gear, but anglers using charcoal or even black Buzz-Bombs have had great success with chums in estuaries. Try painting your favorite jig black and give it a try.

Sockeye fishing and the pioneering effort to solve the mystery of taking this once non-biting salmon on sports gear is described on page 169, "Sockeye Fishing.") The discovery of proper lures and techniques shows the way we can all learn more about fish habits.

Pinks (or humpies) can be taken at river mouths using methods similar to those for chinooks or cohos. Anglers fishing big chinooks at Rivers Inlet in August often find pinks grabbing slow moving, large herring baits.

I also have had great sport there, casting fluorescent red Buzz-Bombs into concentrations of pinks off the mouth of the Kilbella River. Sometimes we got a strike on almost every cast.

Fishing in Spawning Rivers
Many anglers catch salmon after they begin their trek upstream to the spawning beds. If they are taken not too far from tidewater, they are usually good sport and good eating.

Some fishing is done from small boats, but most river fishing is casting from the bank. The techniques are similar in many ways to steelhead fishing. Bait is cast out and allowed to drift downstream near the bottom with the current.

Casting jigging lures from the bank can also be productive. But remember, don't cast to a fishy spot upstream since you will have little control over your lure, let alone a fish.

Try to get the lure to the hot spot when it is between 90 degrees

(straight out) and 45 degrees downstream, and one to two feet off the bottom. If you can elevate yourself above the river, so much the better. Standing on a large rock or high bank will keep more line out of the water and allow for a smoother drift.

When the lure reaches the end of the drift, use short, frequent, lift-drop motions, reeling up slack when the rod is down. Drive the hook home at the slightest "tick" on the line. Retie your line every 10

minutes or every time your lure collides with a rock, cutting off about six inches each time.

Best colors for river fishing, according to Doug Field, are perch (yellow and black), fire orange, chrome, yellow/red, and pink pearl. I like reddish pink in rivers and sometimes paint my white or silver lures with nail polish.

Fall Chinook salmon are taken most readily on salmon egg clusters fished in the same manner as steelhead drift fishing. Jacks (precocious males which spawn at two or three years of age) make up a large proportion of this catch.

Cohos, on the other hand, don't seem to like salmon egg baits. Just as they prefer faster moving baits in the sea, they like more active lures in the rivers. Lures with large spinners seem especially effective.

Spring chinook, the finest of the big salmon, are a special case. These fish leave the sea in early spring (usually March) and do not spawn until fall. They remain in beautiful condition for a long time after leaving the sea. One of the nicest runs of spring chinook head up the Columbia and into the Willamette River near Portland each spring. This run was once close to extinction, but good fisheries management has saved it.

There is growing evidence that scent is extremely effective in river fishing. Anglers using yarn and artificial lures were catching chum and coho salmon in the Nanaimo River and 90 per cent of the fish were being foul hooked or snagged. An angler added Formula X-10 feeding stimulant and was startled when he landed two fished hooked in the mouth. Other anglers added scent, and estimated that up to 90 per cent of the fish were mouth hooked as opposed to 10 per cent without scent. Formula X-10 was developed by Charlie White in conjunction with a researcher at the University of Washington, using ingredients found to increase the feeding behavior of captive salmon.

CHAPTER TEN By Ken McDonald

Sockeye Fishing

For decades sockeye was as neglected by sportsmen as chinook, coho and pink salmon were avidly sought. Tabbed a non-biter, sockeye seemed destined for fame only as the primary supply of canned salmon on the supermarket shelf.

While existing in the millions, sockeye absolutely shunned

sportsmen's offerings. Part of the reason was the sockeye's restrictive diet. A plankton feeder, the sockeye wasn't interested in the big plugs, choice herring and other normal tidbits tossed out by salt-water anglers.

Eventually sportsmen quit trying. "Sockeye don't bite," they said, and that was that. They were wrong, very wrong. In 1967, a revolu-

tion occurred when anglers discovered the secret of catching sockeye.

Early Experiments
The setting was as odd as the revolution. In 1935 the U.S. Federal Bureau of Fisheries hatchery on the Skagit River raised 96,000 fingerlings. They were planted in the Cedar River, a tributary to Lake Washington which is located almost in the heart of Seattle, Washington.

Results from this early plant were disappointing and the effort was more or less given up as a lost cause. Fisheries biologists didn't even bother to check on the progress of the few surviving sockeye.

No one really knows why, but in the late 1950s and early 1960s, the sockeye began to thrive. The number of spawners increased dramatically to a high of 189,400 in 1967. Obviously, annual runs of thousands of sockeye salmon were about to appear. Alerted in 1967 that a record run was due to swim right through the heart of Seattle bound for Lake Washington and the Cedar River, an outdoor publication, *Fishing & Hunting News*, began the sport fishing revolution.

Assured that the sockeye run was permanent, the paper couldn't resist the challenge. All knowledgeable fishery experts, sportsmen and commercial fishermen were consulted. Then the publication set about organizing fishing teams, involving hundreds of fishermen, in a methodical search to develop new, effective fishing techniques and lures.

Poor Results
Early results could by no means be called spectacular. In fact the returns were downright disappointing when compared to the man-hours of effort. But each success added to the reservoir of knowledge these pioneers were building.

Perhaps basic to finding the key to success was cornering the fish. In this case, the fish schooled or milled at the mouth of the Cedar River for up to two months prior to their spawning run.

In Lake Washington, near the Cedar River, it was found that sockeye tended to clump in schools at specific depths. While there was usually some surface activity (sockeye jumping in the water), the majority of the fish frequented a specific level, or layer. In the Lake Washington case, the highest concentration of fish was 35 to 90 feet, with the majority at the 50-foot mark.

Although this grouping level undoubtedly varies in different locations, the researchers discovered that it is important to locate the area of intensity — no problem with modern depthsounders. Once the proper depth is found, it is vital that anglers fish at this depth. In the catch of up to 20,000 sockeye salmon by sports fishermen during the 1973 season, the "proper depth law" was proved again and again.

Developing the Lure and Techniques

Developing the lure and techniques was a matter of trial and error. The paper's editor, Ken McDonald, and publisher Bill Farden stumbled onto one of the secrets during early testing, although at the time the significance of their find was not apparent. Fishing from their 27-foot boat, they twice stopped to pick up fresh-killed sockeye. Each bore a prop cut near its head.

The prop of their boat had recently been chromed and undoubtedly flashed brightly as it revolved. It appeared that sockeye were

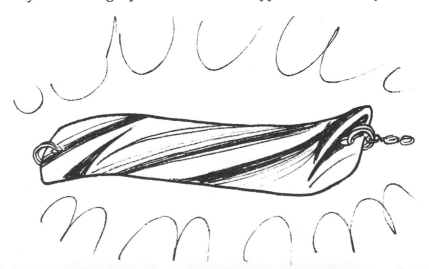

definitely attracted by this flash. Since then a light-reflecting flasher or dodger has proved to be a must for catching sockeye salmon.

There are many brands of flashers on the market, several of the popular ones made in B.C. Chrome flashers easily out-perform the painted dodgers.

Proper lure and depth are the second and third basic ingredients for a successful sockeye outing. When selecting a lure, color is extremely important. Fluorescent red has been deadly, although some other colors have been used with moderate success, one of them silver. The first successful sockeye lure was the fluorescent red U-20

Flatfish. It remains popular. Pink or white hoochies with all but five or six strands torn off are very successful. There are also a number of lures developed specifically for sockeye fishing which are displayed prominently in most tackle shops during the sockeye season.

TYPICAL SOCKEYE RIG

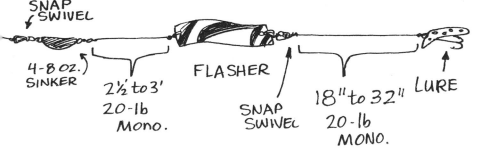

The lure is normally attached to the flasher with 20-pound monofilament and 18-32 inches of leader, with 28-29 inches the most favorable. From dodger to sinker (or diver) another two and one-half to three feet of monofilament is used. Since sockeye have a soft mouth, some anglers use a snubber to ease the shock of the strike.

The third ingredient, depth, is often critical. Forty to 60 feet is usually the most productive, trolling in a zigzag pattern. Sockeye seem to become hypnotized by the flashers moving slowly through the water and schools of them appear to follow almost in formation. For this reason, it is desirable to get your gear back in the water as quickly as possible after playing a fish, or even leave one rod in the water to hold the school.

The rod and reel commonly used for sockeye is usually the same as for other types of salmon. It is seven and one-half feet long, with

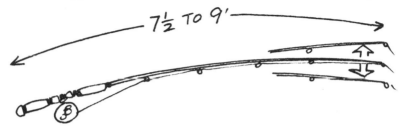

enough strength at the tip to handle the eight ounces of lead that may be used. It must also be flexible since one with too little give will lose many sockeye. As noted, they have a very soft mouth.

The reel can be any style used for fish up to 10 pounds. Capacity should be enough for 200 yards of 20-pound test monofilament, the most popular with sockeye anglers.

Fishing sockeye takes patience since they will not strike a lure trolled at a speed which would be normal for coho or even the heavier chinook. It must be trolled ever so slowly, sometimes utilizing only the drift of the boat for motion. In fact, many anglers report that they did not receive a strike until the lure had completely stopped.

When a five- to 10-pound sockeye strikes there is no doubt about its intention. It strikes viciously and, quite often, flips the hook.

The savage strike lends credence to the theory that the fish is

THAT'S IT! I'VE HAD IT!

striking out of anger. Sockeye certainly do not feed naturally on anything resembling the developed sport gear. In addition, by the time sockeye group in an area, they have usually stopped feeding anyway.

For B.C. anglers, enhancement of the world famous Adams River, the Horsefly River and others is resulting in huge schools of sockeye passing through Johnstone and Juan de Fuca Straits from mid-June to well into August. There are also large sockeye runs up the Alberni Canal on the west coast of Vancouver Island and into some of the inlets at the north end of the Island. The commercial catch has now topped 20 million in a season, with sportsmen's catch expected to rise steadily above the current total of some 100,000.

SURPRISE! WE THOUGHT WE'D DROP BY AND DO A LITTLE FISHING...

MISS SOCKEYE

CHAPTER ELEVEN By Charlie White

Winter Fishing

Many of the techniques and suggestions for the various types of warm-weather fishing also apply to winter trips.

There are, however, certain differences. Your quarry is primarily

CHIP CHIP CHIPPITY CHIP

chinook salmon since cohos are still pretty small. The cohos which will spawn next fall are only 13 to 15 inches and about a pound to a pound and one-half in January. They really don't start to put on weight until about April and more than quadruple their weight in their last six months of life. There is some fishery for small cohos in places such as Saanich Inlet near Victoria and on upper Vancouver Island, with bucktail flies and small spoons the most popular lures. Remember that size limits apply to all species.

Chinooks are active winter feeders and relatively easy to catch if you can get the right lure within easy striking distance. They are hard fighters in the cold water and in prime eating condition. The flesh is almost too full of oil. I find the heavy oil content makes them too hard to smoke, for example, but ideal for barbecuing on a sandwich toaster-type grill in the living room fireplace.

Dress Warmly

Before starting on a winter trip, be sure to dress warmly! Our winters are mild by comparison with most northern areas, but that damp, cool air can be very penetrating on our relatively inactive bodies. Many guests on my boat bundle up from head to knee, instead of from head to toe. They don't realize that feet are the first to get cold. Now I keep an extra pair of insulated boots for those who arrive in their canvas or cloth-covered boating shoes.

Because daylight comes later in winter, there's no need to get up much, if any, earlier than on a normal working day. I schedule my trips to arrive on the grounds about one-half to two hours before slack tide, often in late morning. For this reason I can have a good hot breakfast at home before setting out. Also because crabbing is usually good in winter, I often set my crab trap on the way to the fishing grounds.

Winter Techniques

Winter chinooks move in a pattern which tends to repeat itself year after year. Local knowledge is very important in choosing where to

fish. In my own area off the Saanich Peninsula, salmon gather to feed on the big, mature herring heading into Saanich Inlet and other protected waters to spawn. They lie in the usual hiding places for chinooks — points of land, near abrupt depth changes, and in tidal eddies.

Using downriggers with my depthsounder for accurate control, I put one line at about 50 feet and vary it between 40 and 60 feet. If there is no action, I put another one about 20 feet off the bottom and crank it up and down as bottom contour changes.

Most productive winter lures are herring and various combinations of flasher and flashtail, hoochy, spoon or strip. Rhys Davis, inventor of the well-known Strip Teasers and Herring Teasers, finds

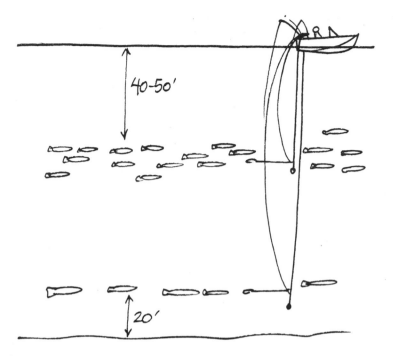

that he catches more winter fish without a flasher. He uses minnows, large seven-inch herring, or large strip in the Sidney area when mature herring are passing through.

A fairly slow troll with a medium speed roll to the herring will usually produce results. Sometimes a faster spin works better, especially when using minnows.

The final pre-production tests of my "The Lure Trolling Model" were made winter fishing where it outfished bait on five out of six occasions. This success convinced us to go into production. But such is the perverse nature of salmon that summer tests were the opposite. We had many trips where herring and anchovies were more productive.

A downrigger and flasher arrangement as already described has proved very successful for winter fishing conditions. The flasher seems to attract salmon from long distances in the clear, plankton-free water, yet it is far enough from the lure itself that they are not spooked. Although many anglers report that flashers seem to scare off the winter chinooks, my combination apparently offers the ideal compromise.

With the generally small and slow-moving tides on winter days, you can fish all day and find fish. My best luck is still during the period from one and one-half hours before slack tide to an hour or two after. Unless there is a lot of action around, I usually get the crab traps and head home well before dark.

While there can be a good bite at dusk, I don't often stay out that late. I want a bit of leeway in case of an accident or a breakdown on the way home. Spending a night on the water in mid-summer is uncomfortable enough. A long, cold winter night is no time to be huddled on a disabled boat.

Speaking of safety, winter boaters should think twice before venturing too far from well protected waters. Storms can come up quickly and violently in the winter, and survival time in the icy water is very short. Stay close to home — the fishing is probably just as good anyway.

*FINI / THE END

Fishing Diary

DATE	TIME	LURE AND COLOR	DEPTH	WEATHER - TIDE

SPECIES - WEIGHT - WHERE

Fishing Diary

DATE	TIME	LURE AND COLOR	DEPTH	WEATHER - TIDE

SPECIES - WEIGHT - WHERE

Fishing Diary

DATE	TIME	LURE AND COLOR	DEPTH	WEATHER - TIDE

SPECIES - WEIGHT - WHERE

More books on B.C. Fishing, Travel, History

According to Federal Fisheries, some 500,000 people go salmon fishing in B.C. every year. An astonishing one-half of them — some 250,000 — don't catch even one fish. Are the successful anglers just lucky? No! Knowledge is their secret.

The following titles will help you catch more salmon, as well as halibut, trout, steelhead, crabs, prawns and other species. In addition, a selection of other books will help you get the most from B.C.'s Great Outdoors.

Available at book, sporting goods stores and other outlets. If not, by mail on the order form on the last page.

HOW TO CATCH SALMON — BASIC FUNDAMENTALS
The most popular salmon book ever written. Information on trolling, rigging tackle, most productive lures, proper depths, salmon habits, how to play and net your fish, downriggers, where to find fish.
The basic book on B.C. salmon fishing with sales over 120,000.
11th printing.

ISBN 0-88792-005-5   *176 pages*   *$5.95*

HOW TO CATCH SALMON — ADVANCED TECHNIQUES
The most comprehensive advanced salmon fishing book available. Over 180 pages crammed full of how-to tips and easy-to-follow diagrams. Covers all popular salmon fishing methods: mooching, trolling with bait, spoons and plugs, catching giant chinook, and much more.

ISBN 0-919214-65-7   *192 pages*   *$12.95*

HOW TO CATCH CRABS
Now in a 10th printing with revisions that show latest crabbing techniques. Tells how to catch crabs with traps, scoops, rings. Where, when and how to set traps. Best baits. Illustrations of a much easier method of cleaning, cooking and shelling the meat. All you need to know.

ISBN 0-88896-133-8   *114 pages*   *$4.95*

and Outdoor Exploration.

HOW TO CATCH BOTTOMFISH

While salmon are the "glamour" fish, bottom fish are tasty and easy to catch. This book shows how to catch cod, sole, perch, snapper, rockfish, and other bottomfish. Best tackle and rigs, baits, when and where to fish. Detailed step-by-step filleting diagrams. Revised and expanded.

ISBN 0-88896-192-8   160 pages $4.95

HOW TO CATCH SHELLFISH

Updated 4th printing of how, when and where to find and catch many forms of tasty shellfish: oysters, clams, shrimp, mussels, limpets. Easiest way to shuck oysters. Best equipment for clamming and shrimping. When not to eat certain shellfish. What to eat and what to discard. A delightful book of useful information. Well illustrated.

ISBN 0-88896-179-0   144 pages $3.95

HOW TO CATCH STEELHEAD

This book by popular outdoors writer Alec Merriman contains helpful information for novice or expert. Information includes how to "read" the water, proper bait, techniques for fishing clear or murky water, and fly fish for steelhead. Many diagrams and illustrations. 4th printing.

ISBN 0-919214-49-5   112 pages $3.95

HOW TO CATCH TROUT

Lee Straight is one of Western Canada's top outdoorsmen. Here he shares many secrets from his own experience and from experts with whom he has fished.
Chapters include trolling, casting, ice fishing, best baits and lures, river and lake fishing methods — and much more.

ISBN 0-88896-145-6   144 pages $5.95

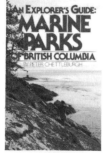

AN EXPLORER'S GUIDE TO THE MARINE PARKS OF B.C.

The definitive guide to B.C.'s 30 marine parks. Includes anchorages and onshore facilities, trails, picnic areas and campsites. Profusely illustrated with color and black and white photos, maps and charts, this is essential reading for all yachtsmen and small boat campers.

ISBN 0-88896-155-3   *200 pages*   *$12.95*

LIVING OFF THE SEA

Detailed techniques for catching crabs, prawn, shrimp, sole, cod and other bottomfish; oysters, clams and more. How to clean, fillet, shuck — in fact everything you need to know to enjoy the freshest seafood in the world. Black and white photos and lots of helpful diagrams.

ISBN 0-88896-152-9   *128 pages*   *$8.95*

SALMON FISHING BRITISH COLUMBIA:
Volume One: Vancouver Island

Vancouver Island is one of the world's best year-round salmon fishing areas. This comprehensive guide describes popular fishing holes with a map of each and data on gear, best time of year, most productive fishing methods and much more.

ISBN 0-919214-73-8   *128 pages*   *$9.95*

SALMON FISHING BRITISH COLUMBIA:
Volume Two: Mainland Coast

Volume Two in this series describes nearly 100 fishing holes from Vancouver up Georgia Strait to Texada Island and Jervis Inlet which have yielded salmon to generations of anglers. Furthermore, they still provide probably the world's most accessible and productive salmon fishing.

Information includes where to fish, gear, best lures, a location map and much more to help turn your reel from "silent" to "sing."

ISBN 0-919214-81-9   *144 pages*   *$11.95*

HOW TO COOK YOUR CATCH

Tells how to cook on board a boat, at a cabin or campsite. Shortcuts in preparing seafood for cooking, cleaning and filleting. Recipes and methods for preparing delicious meals using simple camp utensils. Special section on exotic seafoods. Illustrated.
7th printing.

ISBN 0-88792-017-9   *192 pages*   *$4.95*

HOW TO FISH WITH DODGERS AND FLASHERS

Joined by guest authors Lee Straight, Jack Gaunt and Bruce Colegrave, Jim Gilbert helps you catch more salmon. Find out when to use a dodger or a flasher, all about bait and lure hookups, best lure action, trolling speeds, leader lengths and more.

ISBN 0-919214-47-9   *128 pages*   *$3.95*

DRIFTFISHING: The British Columbia Way

Whether you fish salmon, bottomfish or trout this book of illustrated techniques for mooching, casting and jigging can increase your catch.
Seven expert B.C. fishermen help you become more productive using Perkin, Buzz-Bomb, Stingsilda, Deadly Diok, and herring.
Updated 4th Edition

ISBN 0-88792-011-X   *160 pages*   *$10.95*

FLY FISH THE TROUT LAKES

Professional outdoor writers describe the author as a man "who can come away regularly with a string when everyone else has been skunked."
In this book, he shares over 40 years of studying, raising and photographing all forms of lake insects and the behaviour of fish to them. Written in an easy-to-follow style.

ISBN 0-919214-59-2   *96 pages*   *$7.95*

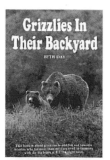

GRIZZLIES IN THEIR BACKYARD
by Beth Day
This book is about grizzlies — and Jim and Laurette Stanton who for more than 30 years lived in harmony with the big bears at B.C.'s Knight Inlet. They considered the abundant grizzlies to be friends, not enemies, even when a mother and her cubs used their garden as a playground.

ISBN 1-895811-16-3   192 pages $14.95

HISTORIC FRASER AND THOMPSON RIVER CANYONS
The Trans-Canada Highway from Vancouver to Kamloops offers scenery from mountains to sagebrush, wildlife from mountain goat to muskrat, vegetation from dogwood to cactus. Here is a mile-by-mile guide — including its colorful history.
Black and white and color photos plus map.

ISBN 0-919214-76-2   128 pages $7.95

Canoe Country British Columbia
BOWRON LAKE PROVINCIAL PARK
by Richard T. Wright
The only ALL-SEASONS guide to North America's unique canoe route ---- interconnected lakes and rivers that form a 116-km-(72-mile-) long circuit amidst the snow-capped peaks of B.C.'s Cariboo Mountains.

ISBN 1-895811-04-X   128 pages $12.95

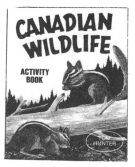

CANADIAN WILDLIFE ACTIVITY BOOKS –
Volumes One and Two
These are educational books for children from 6 to 12. They are not the usual coloring or join-the-dots books but originals which feature illustrations of Canadian wildlife in magazine-size pages. Eachvolume contains over 200 drawings of mammals,birds, fish, reptiles, amphibians and insects.

Volume One ISBN 0-919214-55X 80 pages $6.95
Volume Two ISBN 0-919214-83-5 80 pages $6.95

TYING FLIES FOR TROPHY TROUT

Jack Shaw of Kamloops has spent a lifetime studying the trout for which his region is famous, raising insects in his basement, then tying matching patterns. He explains fly tying from basic equipment to tying 16 productive flies, each illustrated with a one-half page color photo of the insect and a one-half page color photo of the completed fly.

ISBN 0-919214-89-4   144 pages $14.95

GREAT HUNTING ADVENTURES

Like many young boys, Henry Prante's imagination was stirred by tales of big game hunting in the Canadian wilderness. Here he shares his experiences while hunting bear, deer, moose and other big-game species.

ISBN 0-88896-156-1   144 pages $7.95

OUTLAWS AND LAWMEN OF WESTERN CANADA

These true police cases prove that our history was anything but dull. Chapters in 160-page Volume Three, for instance, include Saskatchewan's Midnight Massacre, The Yukon's Christmas Day Assassins, When Guns Blazed at Banff, and Boone Helm — The Murdering Cannibal.

Each of the three volumes in this Canadian best seller series is well illustrated with maps and photos and four-color photos on the covers.
Volume One $9.95; Volume Two $9.95;
Volume Three $11.95

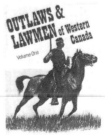

B.C. PROVINCIAL POLICE STORIES: Mystery and Murder from the Files of Western Canada's First Lawmen

The B.C. Police force was born in 1858, the first lawmen in Western Canada. These two popular books relate some of their adventures. All cases are reconstructed from archives and police files by ex-Deputy Commissioner Cecil Clark who served the force for 35 years.

Volume One;   128 pages. $9.95
Volume Two;   144 pages. $9.95
Volume Three;   160 pages. $12.95

Please send me the following books:

Copies	Title	Each	Total
. . . . . .	B.C. PROVINCIAL POLICE STORIES		
. . . . . .	Volume One	$ 9.95	. . . . . .
. . . . . .	Volume Two	$ 9.95	. . . . . .
. . . . . .	Volume Three	$12.95	. . . . . .
. . . . . .	BOWRON LAKE CANOE COUNTRY	$12.95	. . . . . .
. . . . . .	BUCKTAILS AND HOOCHIES	$ 4.95	. . . . . .
	CANADIAN WILDLIFE ACTIVITY BOOK		
. . . . . .	Volume One	$ 6.95	. . . . . .
. . . . . .	Volume Two	$ 6.95	. . . . . .
. . . . . .	DRIFT FISHING	$10.95	. . . . . .
. . . . . .	EXPLORER'S GUIDE TO MARINE PARKS OF B.C.	$12.95	. . . . . .
. . . . . .	FLY FISH THE TROUT LAKES	$ 8.95	. . . . . .
. . . . . .	GREAT HUNTING ADVENTURES	$ 7.95	. . . . . .
. . . . . .	GRIZZLIES IN THEIR BACKYARD	$14.95	. . . . . .
. . . . . .	HISTORIC FRASER-THOMPSON RIVER CANYONS	$ 7.95	. . . . . .
. . . . . .	HOW TO CATCH BOTTOMFISH	$ 5.95	. . . . . .
. . . . . .	HOW TO CATCH CRABS	$ 4.95	. . . . . .
. . . . . .	HOW TO CATCH SALMON – Advanced	$12.95	. . . . . .
. . . . . .	HOW TO CATCH SALMON – Basic	$ 5.95	. . . . . .
. . . . . .	HOW TO CATCH SHELLFISH	$ 3.95	. . . . . .
. . . . . .	HOW TO CATCH STEELHEAD	$ 3.95	. . . . . .
. . . . . .	HOW TO CATCH TROUT	$ 5.95	. . . . . .
. . . . . .	HOW TO COOK YOUR CATCH	$ 4.95	. . . . . .
. . . . . .	HOW TO FISH WITH DODGERS AND FLASHERS	$ 3.95	. . . . . .
. . . . . .	LIVING OFF THE SEA	$ 7.95	. . . . . .
	OUTLAWS & LAWMEN OF WESTERN CANADA		
. . . . . .	Volume One	$ 9.95	. . . . . .
. . . . . .	Volume Two	$ 9.95	. . . . . .
. . . . . .	Volume Three	$11.95	. . . . . .
	SALMON FISHING B.C.		
. . . . . .	Volume One: Vancouver Island	$ 9.95	. . . . . .
. . . . . .	Volume Two: Mainland Coast	$11.95	. . . . . .
. . . . . .	TYING FLIES FOR TROPHY TROUT	$14.95	. . . . . .

Sub-Total . . . .

Postage – Per Book – $1.00 . . . .

GST @ 7% . . . .

Payment can be made by Cheque or Money Order

TOTAL . . . .

HERITAGE HOUSE PUBLISHING COMPANY LTD.
#8, 17921 – 55 Avenue, Surrey, B.C. V3S 6C4

Name (Please Print)

Address

City   **Province**   **Postal Code**